LET THE GOOD TIMES ROLL!

The Complete Cajun Handbook

LET THE GOOD TIMES ROLL!

The Complete Cajun Handbook

ANDY EDMONDS

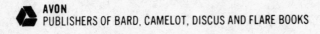
AVON
PUBLISHERS OF BARD, CAMELOT, DISCUS AND FLARE BOOKS

LET THE GOOD TIMES ROLL! THE COMPLETE CAJUN HAND-
BOOK is an original publication of Avon Books. This work has never before appeared in book form.

AVON BOOKS
A division of
The Hearst Corporation
1790 Broadway
New York, New York 10019

First Avon Printing, October, 1984

Printed in the U. S. A.

DON 10 9 8 7 6 5 4 3 2 1

THIS BOOK IS DEDICATED TO CAMELOT, BRIGA-
DOON, AND ALL THE MAGICAL, WONDERFUL,
ROMANTIC PLACES IN OUR WORLD

Acknowledgments

Thanks to Bill Elder of WWL-TV for opening his "vault" and steering me in the right direction, Glen Pitre of Cote-Blanche Productions in Cut Off for being an unlimited source of information and being patient on the phone, Joe Raia for getting me started when I was lost, Mike Sioss for that interesting Cajun barbecue, Wisteria for her generosity and green tea, William Faulkner Rushton for his book, Walter Mouton and Lawrence Patin for a delightful interview at La Poussière, Mom and Dad for reading the rough draft and gluing me to the typewriter, Helene Luft for translating the Cajun stories into English, Mike Hamilburg for his faith and terrific wheeling-dealing, Bill Alexander for his tremendous help and all my newfound Cajun friends for their help, recipes, remedies, stories, and recollections.

Laissez les bons temps rouler!

CONTENTS

There's an old Cajun saying that you can only be Cajun in one of three ways—by birth, by the ring, or through the back door.

Welcome to the back door!

INTRODUCTION

The Bayou

GLISTENING WATER, shimmering in the reflection of a bright afternoon sun. A warm wisp of air accompanied by the peaceful chirp of birds and the distant splash of a marshland animal. Moss-covered cypresses. Winding roads guarded by tired, wooden houses. Swaying pontoon bridges and the clean scent of nature. The Louisiana Bayou. A place where time stands still and a person can indulge in self-reflection.

There's something special and magical about the Bayou. A feel of peace and harmony that is reflected through its people and their attitude toward life, nature, and each other. An openness and inner confidence that few other places have been able to capture or maintain.

Many Cajuns believe that when God declared the seventh day a day of rest, He came down to the Bayou . . . and never left. Just about anyone who spends any time in the Bayou would probably agree. The Cajun people put their trust in three things—God, each other, and nature. In that order. The area certainly seems touched by the hand of God, and it shows in every town, home, and resident.

The Cajuns have weathered violent, devastating acts of nature such as hurricanes, floods, and blight. They've been slaughtered and driven from their homeland in Nova Scotia. Families have been torn apart, children left to die. But each time, their faith in God and strong

15

self-reliance pulled the Cajuns through—each time becoming stronger and more self-assured.

The Cajuns are as unique as the Bayou area they call home. They have their own language, which has been compared to a cross between old French and street slang. They have their own music, their own food, and their own views on nature. Outsiders have fought to destroy the Cajun customs, standardize the language, commercialize the people, and force the Cajuns into the "mainstream." Each time, the Cajuns quietly remain steadfast, with the "outsiders" eventually adopting the Cajun way of life, appreciating its simplicity and gentleness.

The 3500 square miles of Bayou in southern and southwestern Louisiana is home to nearly 1 million Cajuns. The Louisiana legislature has proclaimed the Bayou area "Acadiana" in honor of the Acadians, the Cajuns. The area is composed of 22 parishes (counties), with the city of Lafayette at its heart. The parishes are Acadia, Ascension, Assumption, Avoyelles, Calcasieu, Cameron, Evangeline, Iberia, Iberville, Jefferson, Lafayette, Lafourche, Pointe Coupee, St. Charles, St. James, St. John the Baptist, St. Landry, St. Martin, St. Mary, Terrebonne, Vermilion, and West Baton Rouge. The area stands solidly as "Cajun Country," recognizable by its small, close-knit communities, open and friendly atmosphere, and shops and billboards declaring "authentic Cajun this" and "down-home Cajun that."

One of the most special aspects of the parishes is the unity among them. People from other parishes are considered neighbors and are treated as friends, whether they are right next door, down the block, or across the state. This sense of unity makes the Bayou area one community instead of a smattering of small, isolated towns.

The Bayou area is built around marshes and swamps, with winding roads, moss-covered cypress trees, and thick green underbrush. The towns are small and spread out; the houses are old and quaint. The air is fresh and sweet; the atmosphere is warm and friendly. Southern and southwestern Louisiana are considered "Deep South" in both location and customs. Bordered on the west by Texas, the north by Arkansas, the east by Mississippi, and the south by the Gulf of Mexico, the Bayou blends Southern charm with old-world Cajun tradition.

There's an old-fashioned hospitality among the Cajun people. They are raised according to a strict set of rules governing dating, etiquette, and life-style. The Cajun women are ladies. The men are gentlemen.

Cajuns are friendly, but careful with strangers. They have an inner "sixth sense" about trust. Trust is considered one of the highest honors paid to another, and when a Cajun's trust is won with honesty, a Cajun friend becomes a friend for life.

Although the Cajuns are raised as gentle people, with quiet and polite social conduct, they're also the first to shake loose and kick up their heels at the Saturday night dance, called the fais-dodo. The Cajuns take their fun seriously and live by the motto, "Laisser les bon temps rouler!" Let the good times roll!

Perhaps the best way to understand the Bayou and the Cajuns is through seeing the dichotomy in their existence. The Bayou area is filled with contrast. It's a page out of time; it rambles along at its own pace, surrounded by a fast-moving world. It's an open area in an overcrowded country. The Bayou supports centuries-old customs as a way of life, holds 1 million people, yet remains an undamaged wilderness. In this dichotomy lies the romance and charm of the Bayou.

The romance is carried throughout the Bayou and interwoven through its people, who also live in contradiction, yet manage to keep an even balance between the old and new, maintaining a steady harmony with nature.

A drive across Interstate 10 (the main highway through southwestern Louisiana) highlights the balance of a sleeping past and bustling future. Eighteen miles of concrete-and-steel suspension bridges arch gracefully over algae-choked swamps holding court to a massive graveyard of dead and rotting cypress trees. Modern hotels and brightly colored fast-food restaurants stand shoulder to shoulder with deteriorating wood-frame houses. Teenage boys race down the highway in sports cars, past old men fishing along the marsh with bamboo poles and last night's leftovers.

Traditional industries exist hand in hand with modern technology. For hundreds of years, Cajuns have gathered moss from the swamp-area trees, using it for stuffing chairs and mattresses and for costume decorations. The Cajuns still paddle their pirogues (small, shallow boats) far into the dark Bayou to gather moss by hand. As they paddle back into the main channel, they are greeted by private and commercial fishing vessels, shrimp boats, and massive international cargo ships docked in the Gulf.

A drive through the southern Bayou areas, such as Bayou Lafourche, winds past old, weather-beaten shacks on stilts, barely keeping balance at the water's edge. Next to the shacks are new, expensive ranch-style houses with modern conveniences and two cars in the driveway. There's no rivalry between the neighbors, who are often related. There's no show of "one-upsmanship," no feeling of superiority. In fact, often the family living in the "shack" will be quite wealthy from oil or fishing, choosing to put their money in the bank or reinvest it in the family business.

The southwestern Bayou areas are different from those to the south. The towns are larger, more built up and crowded (a "crowded" Bayou town still looks rural and empty compared with most major cities). Lafayette, one of the main cities, and the center of Acadiana, hosts the University of Southwestern Louisiana, major industries, and commercial businesses. The houses are larger, more uniform; streets are busier, giving more the air of a bustling city than a remote town or village. The two Bayou areas are different in stature, but they share a common ground of charm, grace, and quaintness. Together, the two areas offer a perfect balance.

The Cajun people also have a dichotomy in their spiritual and religious conventions. Cajuns are Catholic by heritage and tradition, with their Catholic roots going back some 400 years to their beginnings in Nova Scotia, then French-ruled Acadia. They're deeply religious, God-fearing people, with a firm and evident faith in Christ and Christianity; Cajuns have died and faced relentless hardships for their religion. Yet many Cajuns openly practice spiritualism and "white magic," are very superstitious, and have customs that skirt the fringes of voodoo. Some of their practices and beliefs are in direct opposition to the teachings of the Catholic Church. The Cajuns hold a steady balance between the two seemingly opposite religious beliefs, blending the Catholic religion with old-world spiritualism.

The most dramatic contrast goes deeper than the landscape or religion. It goes right to the heart of the Bayou. The Cajuns seem to have discovered the secret of successful cohabitation with nature, living side by side in an ideal give-and-take relationship with the Bayou animals and the land. They work with the land instead of fighting it, and have a deep understanding of the animals and their habitat. The Cajuns maintain an even flow with nature that continues full circle, just like the balance between night and day in the Bayou.

During the day, the Bayou comes alive with a flurry of activity and a sense of purpose and direction. The sound of cars pounding against

narrow, potholed roads shatters the silence. Neighbors chat and trade
stories and gossip along backyard fences and frontyard driveways.
People work in fields or factories. Oil wells pump in unison. Children
laugh. Dogs bark, and a flutter of birds breaks the skyline. A Bayou
town seems almost like a typical small-town community going about its
daily routine. The air is filled with sound, movement, and vibration.
There's life throughout the Bayou.

While there's much activity above the surface of the water, animal
life beneath it crawls at a sleepy pace. Crawfish burrow in the muddy
banks. Shrimp creep on the Bayou floor. Alligators plod far into the
steamy Bayou to escape the heat and hunters' clubs. Nutria and armadillos hide in the thick Bayou moss and vegetation. The animals lie
quietly, waiting for the sun to set and their turn to come to life. The
aquatic world of the animals is in balance with the drier world above
the surface.

When the sun finally relinquishes its hold on the Bayou, the moon
glows in the evening sky, and the Cajuns settle in for the night. Slowly,
as if a veil were carefully lifted, the Bayou is reborn in the moonlight.
The steady drone of crickets and other insects replaces the sounds of
humans, filling the calm night air. The water, unbroken by fishing
boats, shimmers peacefully in the darkness, its glassy surface reflecting the moon's golden beams. The animals emerge, crawling from
swampy banks and thick brush, staking their claim on the moss-laden
Bayou. The marsh comes alive with nature—the sound of nature, the
smell of nature, the feel of nature. While the animals come to life, the
people of the Bayou go to sleep. The balance of man and nature in the
Bayou runs full circle and is complete.

Perhaps the final contrast of the Bayou is the land and its people
against the outside world. The Cajuns are friendly and open and have
an air of gentle innocence about them. They seem untouched by time,
yet they are quite modern in their businesses, dress, and views of the
outside world. They are politically aware, yet somehow unconcerned
with the troubles of the world and its uncertain future. The Cajuns still
have a charming, old-fashioned morality and keep a strict sense of
right and wrong. The pace of life seems slower than the pace of the
outside world.

Somehow, though, when the Cajuns put it all together, their life-
style, views, and conduct seem right, and the rest of the world seems
awkwardly out of step. The Bayou is a place to slow down and rest,

nestled in a world that only offers restlessness. The Bayou is a place to which few would consider moving, but once there, few want to leave. The Cajuns make outsiders wish they were privileged enough to be born in an open and innocent land, where the animals roam free, there are no deadbolts on doors, and neighbors really do watch out for and help one another.

The Louisiana Bayou is like no other place in the world. Its charm is natural and its people unaffected. The people seem to have found the real secret to life. The secret is harmony, and with this harmony comes happiness. That is perhaps the Cajun's greatest gift to the world: Laissez les bons temps rouler!

The Acadians

ON THE SURFACE the Cajuns seem to be blessed—living in peaceful coexistence with nature, enjoying life, and looking at the world with a fun-loving, wide-eyed attitude. Cajuns will tell you that their *bons temps* (good times) nature came about only after a very bitter fight for survival . . . a fight the Cajuns came close to losing more than once.

The Cajuns are formally called Acadians, having settled in French-ruled Acadia in the 1500s. Acadia came to be known as Nova Scotia about 100 years later, but the villagers still referred to themselves as Acadians. The early settlers were mainly from several prominent, wealthy French families that immigrated to the area to adopt a new life-style. They became farmers, trappers, and hunters, living off the land and prospering. They lived quietly and worked as a close-knit community, much the same as the Cajuns do today. The Acadian towns grew as more and more French families left their homeland to stake their claim in the Nova Scotia wilderness.

In 1710, after years of seesaw battles between France and England, Grand Pré, one of the strongest Acadian provinces, fell under English rule. England slowly seized control of the remaining Acadian towns, gaining absolute rule over the region in 1713 with the Treaty of Utrecht. As England tightened its grip around the Acadian stronghold, the French-aligned Acadians solidified their stand against English rule. The power struggle became more intense, and England took drastic measures to put down the Acadian rebellion.

The Catholic Church had been banned in England several years prior to the seizure of Nova Scotia. A provision in the Treaty of Utrecht had allowed the Acadians to practice openly the religion of their choice, which was Catholicism. In an effort to gain absolute control over the region, England broke the agreement and enforced the religious ban. It declared the Acadians British subjects, forcing them to abide by the law and swear allegiance to the crown or face exile.

The Acadians maintained their independence and opted to flee their homes. In 1756 more than 6000 French Acadians began an exodus they called "Le Grand Dérangement." Many moved to a remote French settlement called Cape Breton on Royale Isle in Nova Scotia. Suddenly, the once-prosperous mainland, for which England had fought so hard, now faltered. Those who chose to remain behind and pledge loyalty to England found they could not work the land without the help of the Acadians.

In an act of revenge against the uprising, and to stop the remaining Acadians from leaving the region, England declared a terrorist war against the Acadians. Homes were burned without warning, crops and livestock were destroyed, families were tortured and forced to remain against their will.

Even this could not stop the Acadians from following their religious beliefs and French alignment. With nothing left to lose, the Acadians continued to fight. England then dealt the death card to the band of rebels. It ordered the Acadians banished from Nova Scotia.

Although England wanted the Acadians out of Nova Scotia, it refused them permission to flee to Canada or other French provinces, fearing their joining with other French-aligned settlers would make them too strong, creating a more serious uprising in the future. It decided that the rebels should first be punished, then exiled without warning.

That punishment consisted of surprise attacks on forts and villages, attacks that brutalized children and women and continued the pattern of pillage and carnage. When the exile was imposed, Acadians were literally torn from their land, forced to leave all possessions behind. To make certain the troublesome people would not reunite against the crown, Acadian families were separated. All single men were shipped off in one direction, married men in another. Women were sent away from their husbands, children taken away from their mothers.

England had already claimed as its possessions all of New France (the French provinces in North America including Louisiana) and the British colonies in America. As part of the plan to scatter and destroy the families, refugee ships were randomly sent to English territories. Some Acadians survived the ordeal, settling in America, New France, England, and even the West Indies. Many died along the way, never knowing the fate of their loved ones on other ships.

Still others were not able to adjust to the new wilderness areas, or found themselves incompatible with other British subjects because of their now-fierce disloyalty to England and their strong Catholic faith. They chose to return to their Nova Scotia homeland and face whatever problems awaited them.

By this time, it was too late. England was already weary of fighting the rebels and wanted no part of them. In 1760, it ordered the Acadians out or face death. They chose exile for the last time and were sent to America.

In all, some 16,000 Acadians were deported from Nova Scotia. The sudden influx of these strange French people confused and intimidated the early American colonists. When the Acadian ships docked in towns such as Williamsburg, Virginia, the immigrants were refused permission to disembark. Some ships finally went to England, where the Acadians were taken prisoner; most eventually died.

In Pennsylvania, the Acadians were refused entry and forced to remain on their ships during the winter. More than half of those who survived the exile from Nova Scotia died while in port; others went insane. When they were finally allowed to leave the ship, the insane were imprisoned, and the children were made slaves.

History records similar stories in Georgia, the Carolinas, Connecticut, and New York. When the Acadians were temporarily allowed to settle in the colonies, they fought side by side with the colonists against Indian uprisings, only to be considered "French loyalists" when the trouble was over.

Acadians protested their mistreatment to King George II of England, but instead of help, the "solution" was a decree sent to the different justices of New York, imposing slavery on Acadians under 21 years of age. That same year, 1762, similar laws were imposed in other colonies.

While some Acadians were facing imprisonment, slavery, and even death in the American colonies, others who had fled Nova Scotia and escaped deportation had established strong French-aligned colonies in New Brunswick, and some were living in forests in isolated areas of Nova Scotia, especially around Halifax. England again sensed the tide turning against it, and sent in troops to destroy and disperse the colonies. Villagers were maimed, tortured, abused, and starved. Finally resigning themselves, they gave up the battle against England and their stand on religious freedom in their homeland. They fled.

Meanwhile peace was declared in the ongoing war against England and France. By 1762, France had established a strong foothold in a Louisiana port city called New Orleans. For thousands of tired, sick, desolate Acadians, the French town meant refuge among people who spoke their language and understood their religion.

The first Acadian immigrants arrived in New Orleans in the fall of 1763. They were welcomed by the townspeople and were granted land rights along the Mississippi River. Louisiana officials gave the new settlers the necessary tools, seeds, livestock, and shelter to get them established. Soon, Acadians from other American colonies migrated to Louisiana and received similar help and support to farm and settle in the swamps and marshes along the Mississippi. The areas first settled are now called Donaldsonville, Bayou Lafourche, Bayou Plaquemine, the Atchafalaya, and Bayou Teche. Of all these areas, Bayou Teche was the most difficult and last to settle because of savage raids and attacks by the Attakapas Indians, a hostile, cannibalistic tribe.

When England began releasing its Acadian prisoners, they flocked to Louisiana. For them, Louisiana was a tropical paradise where the sun was warm, the vegetation lush, the crops bountiful . . . quite a contrast to their recent hardship and even the brutal winters in Nova Scotia.

England had eased its hold on the imprisoned Acadians while it was losing its grip on the American colonies. The Revolutionary War erupted as the colonists fought to tear loose from England's tyranny. The Acadians, backed by the French, quickly enlisted in the fight against England, offering support, arms, and troops, and eventually playing an important part in the battle for independence. Spain soon joined in the battle, and Spain, France, and the French-aligned Acadians helped force England to release its hold on the 13 colonies.

Several heros emerged from the Revolutionary War. One was the

Marquis de Lafayette, a French nobleman who traded his wealth for a general's uniform after hearing about the French and Acadian participation in the war. Lafayette fought with George Washington and helped turn the course of the war by winning battlefield victories against the English. Lafayette, the heart of Louisiana Cajun country, is named after him.

Another was the Comte de Grasse, admiral of the French West Indies fleet, who inflicted such a heavy toll on the English in Chesapeake Bay that the British fleet was unable to regroup in time to rescue Cornwallis at Yorktown. Grasse's initial victory eventually led to Cornwallis's defeat, giving the colonists the final victory at Yorktown and ending the Revolutionary War.

History often focuses exclusively on the colonists' struggles and battles in the Revolutionary War and New England–area residents sometimes claim the exclusive right to membership in organizations such as the Daughters of the American Revolution. The colonists in no way fought the British alone. In fact, without the help of the Spanish, French, and Acadians, the outcome of the war could have been drastically altered.

Snobbism and false pride are rare in Acadian culture. In keeping with their attitude of nonchalance, most Cajuns prefer to remain quiet about their participation in the war. They are aware, however, that many of the early colonists in New England had been thrown out of England as debtors and undesirables, with the colonies used as a massive prison. The Acadians had been successful French farmers and landowners who chose exile rather than compromise their religious and cultural beliefs. The Acadians fought in the Revolutionary War by choice as an affirmation of their belief in freedom of religion and opposition to English tyranny.

Although the British were soundly defeated in the war, England had not yet had its final say against the rebel Acadians. Louisiana was still a French stronghold (although at this time it was a Spanish territory). Iroquois Indians had received training and ammunition from England, and roamed the Louisiana territory attacking Bayou-area villages without warning. England ordered remaining British officers to Louisiana to lead their Indian allies in bloody raids on the French and Acadians. Acadians were maimed and tortured, villages wiped out, women and children killed. When this last act of vengeance against the Acadians was complete, England ended its rule in America.

Louisiana joined the Union in 1812, the year the last major battle with England erupted. The War of 1812 raged on, and again the Acadians took up arms against the British. Three years later, the final battle of that war was fought in the heart of the Acadian area—New Orleans—and thousands of Acadians fought alongside Andrew Jackson, driving the British out and keeping the city and the Mississippi River from falling into the hands of the British.

Throughout the years, the Acadians have maintained an active part in our country's quest for freedom and independence. They fought solidly in the Civil War, aligned with the South against Northern dictation over their homeland. It was the Acadians' French heritage to some extent that prompted the French to pour money into the United States to help build the early railroad systems. Cajuns fought side by side with the French in both World Wars, and have become a major influence in world trade through their oil exporting and fishing.

The Cajuns have suffered cruelty and near-annihilation at the hands of others. But each time, they have pulled through and survived, rarely passing judgment or blaming others for their ordeals.

One of the most famous tributes to the Cajuns' suffering and survival is *Evangeline,* the 1847 poem by Henry Wadsworth Longfellow. The poem is based on the true story of two Acadian lovers, Emmeline Labiche and Louis Arceneaux, who were separated during the exile from Nova Scotia. In the poem, the lovers Evangeline and Gabriel are to be married, but as the town prepares for the festival, a soldier arrives on orders from the king of England. The king decrees all land and animals confiscated, the Acadians driven out of Nova Scotia, and the town of Grand Pré burned.

The lovers are separated, Gabriel arriving first in America, Evangeline months later, living with Indians, searching for her lost love. After years of searching for Gabriel, Evangeline feels compelled to attend to the sick and dying in a small countryside church. In the church is Gabriel, near death. The two lovers finally reunite, and Gabriel dies in Evangeline's arms. While still holding Gabriel, Evangeline prays a thankful prayer, then resigns herself to death to be with Gabriel at last. The poem ends with the two lovers buried side by side in unmarked graves behind the old church.

The true story is slightly less romantic and poignant, with Emmeline searching her whole life for Louis, only to find him resting under an oak tree, married to someone else. Emmeline died alone and lonely, never finding happiness.

In the mid-1800s, St. Martinville resident Edward Simmons related the true story of Louis Arceneaux and Emmeline Labiche to his Harvard professor, Nathaniel Hawthorne. Hawthorne thought the end of the story was too harsh and anticlimactic, and bowed out of writing the story. Longfellow heard the tale, and believed it could be altered slightly to become a great love story. *Evangeline* quickly became popular and is now considered a literary masterpiece.

In 1929, Delores Del Rio starred in the silent-movie version of *Evangeline*. She was reportedly so touched by the story, the plight of the Acadian people, and their warm hospitality that she donated a bronze statue of Evangeline, dedicating it to the Acadian people and Emmeline Labiche. The statue now marks the grave of Emmeline in the cemetery of St. Martin de Tours Church in St. Martinville.

The Cajuns have weathered savage attacks and fierce battles for freedom. They have also faced, and won, the test of strength against nature.

When the Acadians first arrived in Louisiana, they were neither equipped nor prepared for life in the newfound tropical paradise. In Nova Scotia, they were farmers, raising livestock and crops during the summer and living off their harvest during the freezing winter months. They learned to live by the seasons, much as U.S. farmers do in the Midwest today.

Louisiana is swampland with a mild climate. Early Acadians had a difficult time adjusting, even with the help of Louisiana officials who gave them tools, seeds, and housing. But once they dug deep and took hold of the land, they turned the vast marshland into a highly productive area for lumbering, rice, soybeans, cotton, and sugarcane. They even learned to fish for strange-looking animals called crawfish and turned the fishing business into a major Louisiana industry.

The Cajuns learned to work in conjunction with the land, but they have occasionally faced devastation and almost complete annihilation by nature—floods and hurricanes that have killed thousands of men, women, and children.

One of the most destructive hurricanes that lashed through the Bayou was in 1909, when hundreds of Cajuns drowned and most of the southern Bayou was left in shambles. One 85-year-old Chauvin-area woman remembers the hurricane, and how, as a little girl, she helped save her family while others around her drowned. Here is how she remembers the disaster.

The skies were dark and I knew it was going to be a bad storm. I was across the way helping some neighbors take care of their baby. I knew I had to get home, and get someone to come and see about the baby. . . . It was a little road, oh about so big, and my friend she say, "Oh, you're not going to go by yourself!" I said I had to. There were no lights then, and all the animals were making noise, howling at the storm. The wind was blowing real bad now. So I said, "Dear God be in front of me, Mary in back of me." I took my rosary and walked down the road sprinkling Holy Water in front of me, blessing the road. . . . My mama and daddy cried when I got home; they thought I was drowned in the water. . . . Well, I told my daddy, I said, "Let's go in the boat, the big storm is getting thick." By this time everything was falling. . . . The cloud was so black and it was moving so fast. It's very ugly. The wind was coming and it was a black sea. Just as black as coal. I said to my daddy again, "Dear Daddy, please do as I ask and let's go in the boat." . . . My mama and daddy and the babies, we all got in and put blankets around ourselves. . . . The wind broke our kitchen . . . broke it right down . . . took our stove away. So we were in the boat praying. My mama was starting to make a miscarriage and she was getting weak. Then the storm broke our rope that tied our boat to the tree and we went adrift. We went way down the Bayou to the swamp. Not a glass on the boat broke; but people around us were hollering and dying. My daddy, he said, "Dear daughter, every time you tell me something from now on, I listen" . . . because we were all safe because of God. For six miles on each side of the Bayou, they didn't have a house left. Whole families drowned together. They never found half of those people that got drowned, you see. It was horrible, but my mama, daddy and the babies, we were all safe."

A hurricane in the early 1920s again wiped out most of the southern Bayou. The skies blackened; the usually calm, shallow water swelled to 14 feet high, knocking down the small wooden Bayou homes and leaving few survivors in its wake. Those who did survive say they managed either to cling to driftwood or rafts or to rope themselves to trees against the current. When the water receded, the survivors buried their dead and slowly pieced their shattered lives back together.

The Cajuns are not people to give up any sort of battle, no matter how serious the consequences, if they believe they are right. They are not about to walk away from their land and declare nature the winner. After each devastating hurricane, each flood, the Cajuns pitch in and help pull others through. Together, they work to get back in step, reclearing the land, planting new crops, beginning new farms. The Cajuns had found their niche in nature and established a firm hold on their land. Some years ago, however, they found themselves facing yet another destructive force, an enemy they thought they had settled with long before.

That "enemy" was another group of humans who tried to control the Cajuns. As the Cajuns successfully worked the land, raising cotton, sugarcane, and rice, and established prosperous ranches, wealthy combines flocked to the Bayou and tried to cash in on the Cajuns' hard work. Some families sold out; others were driven off their land by pressure and strong-arm tactics. The pattern was always the same—a family would buy or homestead a small piece of swampland, establish a successful crop or herd, and then outsiders would force them from the land. The Cajuns would move on, only to face eviction again.

The pattern continued until the 1920s, when the Cajuns found their land was rich with oil. When word got around the Bayou and spread to the outside world, a wave of greedy oilmen and oil companies swept through the Bayou, buying up or outright stealing the oil-rich land from the Cajuns. This was the final straw for the Cajuns, who decided they had had enough. They banded together, standing up against the oil companies and holding firm on their land. Eventually, the oil companies were forced to reckon with the strong-willed Cajuns, and found ways to work with, not against, the people. Although the Great Depression was on, the joint effort by the companies and the Cajuns kept the Bayou afloat, and many Cajuns enjoyed record prosperity during this hard economic time.

Today, many Cajuns are wealthy landowners, farmers, and ranchers, and they own fishing and shrimping fleets, oil fields, and oil cargo ships that trade in foreign waters.

The Cajuns are proud of their heritage, but they have fought hard for that pride. For nearly 200 years, the Acadians were considered outcasts and driven from their land in Nova Scotia and the United States. They were looked down on because of their unique Cajun-French language and old-world customs. When the Cajuns gained the attention of the outside world through their farming and oil fields, they began to feel self-conscious about their differences. They felt awkward and were considered by some to be "poor white trash" because of their unusual speech and rural life-style. Children were not allowed to speak Cajun-French. Over the past two generations, the Cajun culture and language slowly began to die. Today, the language is almost dead, but efforts are being made to revive it. Schools are teaching French, and the Cajuns are once again proud to be Cajun.

In spite of all the hardships, all the tragedies, all the suffering and setbacks inflicted by both man and nature, the Cajuns have kept their warm, easygoing, "bons temps" attitude. Instead of getting sullen and bitter, the Cajuns seem to bounce back from each tragedy and continue life as usual. One Cajun summed it up this way, "When you've seen the worst and been down so long, just about every day living seems good. We've got God. We've got life. We've got each other. So all we can do is make the best with what we got. We enjoy life because, really, that's all any of us got!"

The Acadian Flag

THE ACADIAN FLAG is the official flag of the Acadians of Louisiana and is flown throughout the region next to the U.S. flag.

The flag first came into recognition in 1965, in accordance with the 200th anniversary of the arrival of the first Acadians in Louisiana. It was officially designated the flag of Acadiana in 1974.

The flag consists of three parts—gold star, fleurs-de-lis, and a gold tower. The gold star on a white field has two meanings. First, it is a reminder of the Acadians' and Louisiana's participation in the Revolutionary War. During the war, Louisiana was a Spanish colony, serving under José Galvez, the governor of Spanish Louisiana. Because the territory had not yet been made an official part of the United States, its star could not appear on the first American flag. Therefore, the gold star on the Acadian flag is the star that was "left out" of the first flag. Second, the star is the symbol of the Virgin Mary. King Louis XIII of France had declared Mary the "Patroness of the Kingdom" and consecrated France and its colonies to Mary in 1638.

The three fleurs-de-lis, which are silver on a blue field, symbolize the French origin of the Acadians, and are also a portion of the arms of France. This section of the flag ties the Acadians' allegiance to their "Mother Country."

To symbolize the Acadians' appreciation to Spain for its participa-

31

tion in the Revolutionary War, and for first offering the exiled Acadians refuge and opportunity, the flag bears a gold tower on a red field. The tower was the symbol of the arms of Castile of Spain.

The red, white, and blue fields of the flag, the colors of the U.S. flag, symbolize the Acadians as Americans.

LIFE-STYLE

Trapping, Hunting, and Fishing

IMAGINE WALKING ALONE, along the water's edge, forging your way through the thick, dark Bayou vegetation. You push aside moss hanging from cypress trees. You hear something rustling in the plants at a distance. Suddenly, a flock of birds shoots through the air, screeching. The rustling sound moves closer and closer. You stop and feel something poking at your heels. You turn around, look down, and find a weird and eerie sight: a 25-pound brown rat with twinkling eyes, a foot-long tail, and huge Dumbo ears. You've just come face to face with one of the most unusual creatures in the Bayou. You've just met your first nutria.

The Bayou is filled with all sorts of strange animals—muskrats, armadillos, and mink, along with more "conventional" animals, such as white-tailed deer, rabbits, quail, snipes, black bears, and of course alligators. The Bayou is a hunter's paradise where the animals roam free and in abundance.

The fur-trapping industry in Louisiana is big business. In fact, 40 percent of all wild fur sold in the United States is trapped in Louisiana, bringing in some $10 million each year for Bayou-area hunters and trappers. Nutria, used for everything from fur coats to pet foods and food for mink, is the biggest of the wild-fur businesses. Some 95 percent of all nutria in the world comes from the southern and southwestern Bayou. Nutria is now Louisiana's major fur export, shipped to all parts of the world.

One of the most surprising things about nutria is that the odd-looking creature isn't even a native of Louisiana. A Cajun named E. A. McIlhenny originally brought some of the animals from South America to his Bayou ranch in 1937. He thought he could raise the nutria for their fur because they were hearty and larger than mink and muskrat. He filled his ranch with nutria pens and cornered the market (mainly because no one else in the Bayou believed there was a future in nutria).

The nutria prospered without much fanfare until 1940, when a hurricane swept across the Bayou, scattering the nutria pens across the swamps. The nutria went wild, literally, and before long the 300 original nutria multiplied to 3000. At first, hunters and trappers were ecstatic with the idea of these big fur-bearers roaming wild because they thought the nutria would breed with the mink and muskrats, ending up with the world's biggest mink pelts. Unfortunately, things didn't turn out quite like they expected; the nutria began killing the other animals for food and taking over the land.

Now the funny-looking rats were out of control, and there was only one thing left to do: get rid of them. State officials put a bounty on the creatures, offering a reward to anyone who brought in a nutria pelt, or even a paw, just to prove the animal was dead. The bounty helped, but the nutria were still taking over the Bayou and populating the swamps at a startling rate.

So, with a typical nonchalant Cajun attitude, Bayou hunters and trappers found it was better to work with the animals than to fight them. They developed a process to soften the coarse nutria fur, making it suitable for coats and fur collars. Gradually, the nutria that had plagued the Bayou became one of the main sources of revenue for the Cajun people. Nutria pelts now bring in a competitive market price, and nutria coats are in demand, especially with the recent protests over the use of other wild-animal pelts.

Catching nutria isn't all that easy. It's done with elaborate traps placed at just the right spot. Many trappers set the rigs at what they call nutria runs—the places where the animals run in and out of the

Bayou water. A trap has metal jaws that snap shut when the nutria works its way inside. A good day's work, with about 40 traps, brings in 25 to 30 nutria. Buyers are picky; they usually won't take any animals less than 33 inches long and pay 75 cents to a dollar for each pelt.

Trapping is a tough way to earn a living. First, it's dependent on the world economy and the worldwide market value for fur coats. Second, outsiders often steal nutria traps, leaving Cajun trappers with no means for catching more nutria, unless, of course, they choose to sink their savings back into new traps, only to have them stolen once more.

Fortunately, the doors have reopened on another Bayou-area business that made the swamps famous—alligator hunting. Probably no animal is more closely associated with the Louisiana Bayou and the steamy, algae-covered swamps than the alligator. Alligator hunting was so popular not too long ago that officials banned it altogether. The craze for alligator shoes, handbags, and luggage all but died off. During the ban, the alligators repopulated the steamy back-Bayou. Their numbers have grown enough that hunting is now permitted during the summer months.

Cajun hunters are fair sports and enjoy an even contest with their prey. Catching alligators is probably the ultimate contest between the animals and the Cajuns. Instead of just going out and shooting the 'gators, Cajuns use several unusual methods—some based on trickery, others based on skill and luck.

At night, hunters paddle out into the swamps in their shallow boats called pirogues. Using a method they call "shining," the Cajuns shine a bright light into the alligator's eyes, temporarily blinding it. While it's blinded, the hunters either club it to death or wrestle it first for sport, then drag it into the boat.

During the day, the Cajuns take the direct approach, and venture into the swamps on foot, carrying a long, heavy pole and ax. Because the alligators like to cool off in the heat, they bury themselves in the swampy marsh vegetation, keeping very still, blending in with the scenery. Hunters thump the ground looking for alligator dens or the 'gators themselves. When the alligator comes alive and gets ready to fight, the Cajuns go "one on one" using the poles, eventually clubbing or axing the 'gator. Cajun hunters also try to lure the creatures out by mocking the alligator's cry, which sounds like a mixture of a whale's moan and a dog's howl.

One of the strangest ways some Cajuns catch alligators is with the help of another strange Bayou animal—a Bayou chicken. A Bayou chicken isn't really a chicken, but no one seems to know what kind of an animal it really is. It looks like a skinny, white pelican with a long, slender throat. Cajun hunters hang the Bayou chickens from long, sharp hooks, then suspend the hooks about a foot above the water. The alligators snap at the chickens, spear themselves on the hooks, and dangle until the hunters paddle by and cut down their catch.

With alligator hunting declared legal once again, alligator recipes are regaining their popularity in the Bayou. Alligator steaks, sauces, and dressings are featured in just about every Bayou-area bar and restaurant. Tasting like a cross between chicken and steak, alligator is a Bayou specialty that adds to the mystique and lure of the Bayou.

Stories and legends have grown around the mysterious alligators. Outsiders hear about strangers wandering through the Bayou and never coming out again, presumably eaten alive by alligators. Alligators look fierce and threatening, but what really makes them appear frightening is their seemingly nonchalant attitude. Alligators lie quietly and wait. To outsiders who are not accustomed to 'gator ways, the alligators seem like monsters, waiting to attack.

Cajuns just shake their heads and smile at the stories of their alligators. You probably won't get a straight answer out of a Cajun when asked if the legends of the 'gators are true. Cajuns will let you find out for yourself. All they'll do is tell you to be careful and not to tangle with the 'gators. Their outwardly casual appearance and attitude just might be hiding a lot of emotion underneath.

Although settled, the Bayou is considered by many to be the last untamed wilderness in the United States. The game is plentiful; the swamps and the land have remained virtually untouched and unaltered. The Bayou is one of the few places where a hunter can travel into the dark recesses of nature and see no human traces . . . even though the hunter is probably only a few miles from a large town.

The Bayou is a hunter's paradise for otters, muskrats, wild duck, geese, marsh hens, and another one of those strange Bayou creatures known as water chicken (or "poot" as the Cajuns call it). The water chicken looks different from the Bayou chicken in that it is black and the Bayou chicken white.

More than one-third of all U.S. marshland is located in Louisiana, and it attracts nearly half of all wild-game hunters. Professional and weekend hunters from all over the United States travel to the Bayou and stay in camps to rough it and hunt the wild game. Some camps, which offer little more than a one-room cottage with some old beds and an old stove, charge as much as $100 per night. Most of the rooms are booked in advance during hunting season, as hunters enjoy the chance to mingle with the great outdoors, get close to nature, and fend for themselves in the swampy Bayou country. Of course, the Cajun guides remain close by, making sure the animals never quite get the upper hand on their adventure-hungry guests.

Some foolish or unequipped hunters have been lost in the Bayou. Cajuns say those who wander in without a proper guide, or with delusions of going "one on one" with nature, or looking for trouble, usually get what they deserve. Movies have been made about outsiders poking around the Bayou, or going in to track down some Cajun, and never coming out. Cajuns say those outsiders—or any outsiders who go where they don't belong—probably got eaten alive by alligators, or drowned among swamp moss, or are still wandering around aimlessly, looking for a way out.

Of course, Cajuns know their way around the Bayou, and only they know if those stories are really true, or are just more of the Cajun tall tales that add to the mystique and lure of the Bayou. A Cajun won't let you in on the truth, only wink, smile . . . and leave you with the friendly warning, "Jus' be careful, my fran. De bayous ain't no place fer strangers."

Cajuns love to tell stories, and Cajuns seem to have a story for just about anything. One of their favorite tall tales is how the Bayou came to be filled with a weird sort of crustacean that looks like a mutant lobster.

"Well, my fran. You see eet was like dees. Der were dees lobsters, dey stuck by us Cajuns when we were back der in Nova Scotia. When we was moved out, the lobsters, you see, dey followed us. For miles and miles, lobsters crawled across da ocean after us Cajuns. Well, de journey was so long and difficult, de lobsters weared themselves out . . . getting smaller and smaller. And dat, my fran, is how we get crawfish."

Crawfish, crayfish, stonecrab, Dixie lobster, creekcrab, crawdad, mudbugs, or mudpuppies, the odd-looking, tiny lobsters are the trademark of the Cajuns. No cookbook or restaurant menu would be complete without crawfish. They are an important part of the Cajun culture, from major crawfish festivals, to crawfish-eating contests, to crawfish exporting and fishing industries. Ninety-nine percent of all the crawfish in the world comes from Louisiana. And it's the Bayou's proudest export.

An average person could probably eat 100 or so of the salty mudpuppies. They're usually served piled on a huge plate, so you tend to feel slightly gluttonous at first. After you start getting into the pile, you realize that it takes some work to break off the little tails and pick out the meat. Before long, that pile of crawfish begins to look like the appetizer.

Some 60,000 acres of swampy, muddy land are devoted to the raising and processing of crawfish. Forty crawfish-processing plants in Louisiana clean, sort, and ship some 29 different species. The most common crawfish is about as long as an average man's index finger; half is the tail, where the "meat" is buried. They vary in color, but the most popular is dark red.

Although crawfish is commonplace in Louisiana, it is considered a delicacy in some parts of the world, such as Europe, and a pest in areas such as Hawaii, Australia, and Japan. In Scandinavia, crawfish is expensive, and a serving of only five is considered a treat. And there, crawfish is served boiled, without any sauce or dressing. In Finland, 5000 in one season is considered a good catch. In Louisiana, 5000 is just about what one fisherman will haul in a day in the Atchafalaya Basin.

A good or bad crawfish season depends on the weather. The animals bury themselves in the mud in marshes and swamps, just below the surface. A stormy season with lots of flooding means lots of mud for crawfish, and that means ideal conditions of mating, resulting in a productive crawfish season.

There's definitely an art to catching crawfish. A careless outsider who tries to grab one by hand is likely to get a finger pinched. The crawfish burrow deeper and deeper into the mud when they sense someone on the way. Cajuns use crawfish traps, which look like tubes made out of chicken wire. The traps are baited with minnows or other small fish and submerged just below the waterline in the swamp. The crawfish wander in for the food, but cannot crawl back out because of a one-way wire door.

Cajuns also paddle their shallow pirogues through rice fields and marshes, looking for the crafty animals. A small crawfish net drags behind the boat, stirring up the water, and catching the crawfish as they tumble into the net. In keeping with the Cajun tradition of making good use out of the land, and in keeping with the Cajun philosophy of harmony in nature, Cajun fishermen work with Cajun farmers, using the flooded rice fields for growing crops as well as for raising crawfish. So far, this partnership has been successful and prosperous.

Peeling crawfish takes time to learn, and outsiders have quite a struggle at first. The heads are snapped off, leaving a small, curled tail to contend with. The tail is then snapped in half, the shell peeled back, and the inch or so of salty, chewy meat picked out. It can take an outsider anywhere from 45 seconds to a minute to wrestle with and beat one small crawfish. A whole mound of crawfish peels down to only a fistful of food and some pretty sore fingers. But with a little practice, a crawfish can be ready to eat in a second or two. Some Cajuns are so fast at peeling the crawfish, and have the technique so mastered, that they peel and eat with one hand, while grabbing for the next one with the other.

A cousin of the crawfish is a more common animal—the crab. The only thing common about Bayou crabs is the name. Cajuns say their crabs are bigger and sweeter than others, and that is definitely because of the magic in the Bayou. According to Cajuns, all animals grow bigger, and just about everything's sweeter in the swamp. Few would argue.

Unlike others who raise crabs for a living and have special "farms" and pens, Cajuns try to keep their industry more of a sport. The crabs roam loose in the Bayou, where they have a fighting chance against crabbers. Cajuns go crabbing in the summer, when the crabs are in season and at the peak of their population, but only at night because the hot Bayou sun would quickly kill the crabs that might venture out and snap for bait. The heat would also spoil the crabs already caught, making them impossible to sell or eat.

Cajuns go crabbing in two ways. The more commercial fishing companies use heavy rope nets dragged by ships moving slowly across the Bayou, scooping crabs off the swamp floor. Sometimes, if the crabs are especially stubborn, the ships hang a long, heavy chain in front of the nets. This "tickle chain" jiggles around kicking up mud and snapping at the crabs, making them jump off the floor and into the nets. Cajuns also use the tickle chain and nets to catch shrimp. In shallow water, where ships can't ease in, or the moss and algae are too thick, Cajuns wade through the water, dragging the nets by hand.

Cajuns also go crabbing in another strange but nonetheless typical way. Never wasting anything, Cajuns save the necks from Bayou chickens and use them as bait, much the same way they catch 'gators. They string the necks on small hooks and hang them on the surface of the water, or just below, depending on how deep the water is. When the crabs snap at the necks, their claws get hooked. Cajuns then paddle out and collect the crabs.

Fresh oysters are one of the staples of the Louisiana Bayou. Department stores often set up oyster bars on Fridays, and you'll see hearty Cajun men and women gulp down one oyster after another. With a squeeze of lemon and a dash of Tabasco sauce, oysters are second only to crawfish in popularity. It's difficult to find a restaurant in the Bayou that doesn't offer fried oysters, baked oysters, or raw oysters on the menu. A good Cajun lunch is a plate of crawfish, a half-dozen raw oysters on the half shell, and an ice-cold glass of beer. Cajuns use oysters, and oyster juice, in all sorts of recipes, from oyster pies to stews, jambalaya to gumbo.

As expected, oysters grown in the Bayou are nothing like conventional, store-bought oysters. The magic of the Bayou water makes the oysters more meaty and sweeter than others. They only come in two sizes—large and huge, large being the length of an average man's palm. And when eaten in the Bayou, they taste even better. Cajun's can't explain why and don't even try. They say they don't find many pearls in their oysters because every oyster is a gem in itself. Pearls develop when the oysters become irritated, and how could anything possibly become irritated living in the Bayou? That's Cajun philosophy.

Cajuns have been frogging for centuries, but frog legs have taken a long time to become popular. Frog legs taste like sweet, tender chicken, and Cajuns usually prepare them sautéed in wine sauce. Because the frog population in Louisiana is somewhat limited, frog legs are still considered a delicacy. Usually only the better, more expensive restaurants offer frog legs or frog sauce piquante, a spicy sauce made from the backs and legs of Bayou frogs.

Frogs are a little quicker than other Bayou-area animals, and the Cajuns have to sneak up on the "moss hoppers" in order to catch them. Cajuns go frogging at night, when the water is still and the frogs are resting peacefully in the heavy Bayou moss along the banks. They quietly sneak up on the frogs and try to grab them either with their bare hands or with nets. When bagged, the frogs are dropped into a small wooden box or canvas bag, and then placed in an ice chest to keep them fresh. Cajuns can only go frogging for a month or so at the beginning of summer when the frog population is at its peak, the weather has not yet gotten too hot, and the frogs have not yet migrated deep into the Bayou.

The most popular Bayou animal, at least to outsiders, is the shrimp. Shrimp is one of the best-loved seafoods around the country, if not the world, and quite a bit of it comes from Louisiana. It shouldn't come as a shock to learn that Bayou shrimp are not those tiny cocktail shrimp served as an appetizer. Bayou shrimp are those large $15-a-pound creatures commonly called prawns. Of course, when eaten in the Bayou, prawns are a lot less expensive and a whole lot fresher than store-bought.

When you buy shrimp in waterside fishmarkets, they're usually sold with the heads still attached, which is quite a sight at first. Shrimp have 6-inch-long antennae, beady eyes, and sharp, pointed faces that can give you a good-sized cut if you're not careful. Cajuns eat shrimp much the same way they eat crawfish—by the plateful. They break off the heads, peel, and eat with plenty of lemon and hot sauce. The only difference is that shrimp are easier to peel—and of course you don't have to eat 50 to feel full.

Cajuns catch shrimp about the same way they catch crab, except there are more shrimp boats in the Bayou than boats specifically set up for crabbing. Boats drag lines and "tickle chains," then scoop up the day's catch for marketing. Two types of boats shrimp in the hot sun out in the Bayou: the big, commercial shrimping fleets, and the small, private wooden shrimp boats. The two play a cat-and-mouse game with each other—the smaller boats darting among the bigger shrimpers, trying to scoop up their day's catch before the shrimpers roll through and clean off the bottom of the Bayou.

Most of the shrimping is done deep in the southern Bayou, in an area called Bayou Lafourche, where the shrimpers have access to the Gulf of Mexico and plenty of room to dock the larger boats after the day's catch. The Bayou area is dotted with small restaurants and family-style bars offering the best fresh jumbo shrimp in the world.

The animals that dwell near and in the Bayou water are hunted and killed by the Cajuns, but only for food or other useful purposes. Few animals are killed for sport. And once killed, nothing goes to waste; Cajuns use leftover pieces for bait or rework them into stews and sauces.

Cajuns take their hunting and fishing seriously, and do it as quietly and naturally as possible. In fact, many Cajun men spend the afternoon sitting along the bank of the Bayou, dangling a crooked pole in the water, fishing more for relaxation than sport. You'll rarely see motorized boats speeding through the Bayou, disturbing the natural flow of the water and upsetting the habitat of the animals.

Cajuns have a special, personal relationship with the Bayou animals. They understand the animals' individual natures, know each animal's habits, and know when and when not to hunt. They try not to disturb the delicate balance of nature by depleting the animal population.

Farming

IF IT WEREN'T FOR THE MILES and miles of winding, narrow Bayou marshes and swamps, you'd probably think you were right back in the Midwest, down on the farm. Cows grazing, sheep roaming the countryside, tractors pulling flats through rows of soybeans. Off in the distance, you see a farmhouse and a barn, a rusty swing set, and a small garden.

Louisiana is part of the southern farm belt, where the soil is rich and the temperature is mild. Farmers raise cattle, hogs, sheep, and chickens for both commercial and private consumption. Cotton, soybeans, sugarcane, and rice grow throughout the marshes. The area is one of the most continually bountiful and produces at an even pace, usually unaffected by the drastic temperature changes and sudden freezes that sometimes plague the rest of the South.

The Cajuns raise a lot of cattle, one of the major forms of livestock (along with pigs) to be raised successfully by the early Acadian settlers. The first cattle were Spanish longhorn imported from Mexico and shipped to the early Cajun ranches, called "vacheries." Early Cajun farms were usually not run very tightly, and cattle often wandered in and out of the ranches of the Bayou. Fences were built in those days to keep stray cattle out, not to hold cattle within the property lines. (Even today, Cajuns don't believe in fencing their property, in keeping with the Cajun philosophy of friendliness and openness.) Cattle often

45

grazed their way from one ranch to the next, ending up munching peacefully in someone's flower bed or backyard vegetable garden. This free-ranging style of cattle ranching was probably learned from the local Avoyelles Indians, who successfully raised herds in the open territory.

Major slaughterhouses were located in New Orleans, and many trails went through Breaux Bridge, over the Atchafalaya Basin, down the Mississippi, to Baton Rouge, and then onto cattle boats. Other trails headed more to the south near Morgan City, through Plaquemine, and to the Mississippi. Washington, now mostly noted for its mansions and antiques, was also a major cattle-shipping city in those days before the Civil War. As the cattle trails stabilized, the routes became more and more direct, and shipping became easier and faster. The ranchers became wealthy as the Bayou area gained recognition as one of the major cattle-ranching regions of the South.

Today, the southern and southwestern Louisiana Bayou is the major cattle-producing area of the state. Most cattle are raised for their beef, which is considered some of the most tender in the South. Bayou cattle are also used for stud in other parts of the country and the world, especially South America, where stud bulls are in demand. About one-fourth of the cattle raised in the Bayou are dairy cows, with a large dairy in Abbeville supplying most of the region's dairy products. Major slaughterhouses and meat companies are located in southern Louisiana or have branches in the area, along with many major southern dairies.

The Bayou is ideal for another business—rice farming. Its swamps and marshes, high water level, and frequent flooding give perfect conditions for rice paddies, which have kept the area booming during rough times. In the early days, just about every Acadian farmer had a small rice paddy in the yard along the banks of the Bayou. Farmers tossed rice into the swamp, and it grew with little effort or care. When the grain came up, farmers waded in the swamps and cut it down by hand, then rough-processed it in the barn through a sifter and board. The farmers bagged their crop and sold it in local stores, shipped it to New Orleans via the cattle trails, or ground and milled it themselves for home consumption or feed for chickens and livestock.

When the railroads began etching their way through Louisiana, the cattle and rice industries flourished, shipping was easy, and the area's reputation for farming and ranching spread across the state. More people flocked to the region, and the Bayou soon became dotted with prosperous farms and ranches.

Along with the prosperity came other successful industries, including hog raising and cotton farming. The Acadians always raised hogs, but usually for personal consumption and trade. With the influx of money and outside ranchers, the hog-butchering business grew. Slowly, raising hogs emerged from a backyard sideline to a major industry.

The influx also meant new and more productive methods for growing and picking cotton. Cotton is a major crop throughout the South, and was first picked by hand, bagged, and shipped to local mills for cleaning, stranding, and processing. As more Southerners flocked to the Bayou area, they brought the skill and knowledge for successful cotton farming, and taught their tricks and techniques to the Cajuns. After the Civil War, new and faster methods of picking and processing were developed, and cotton farms grew and flourished throughout the state. Today, the southwestern Louisiana cotton fields are some of the most prosperous in the South, with local cotton mills producing a large percentage of the cotton products for the entire South.

Today, the southern and southwestern part of Louisiana is self-sufficient, raising enough crops and livestock to meet the needs of its own people, as well as leaving an abundant surplus to feed and clothe a good portion of the South. The Cajun people have established their reputation as farmers and ranchers, rising from early stereotypes as backwoods people to recognition as hardworking and industrious people who turned swampland into rich and productive land.

Cooking

CAJUNS EAT AS THEY LIVE—hearty and happy. They use food as the basis for social gatherings, or to welcome strangers and make them feel right at home. Not many people will argue with the claim that Cajun cooks are among the best in the world. Cajuns blend the best of two cultures, French and Southern country, and end up with some recipes that are out of this world.

Cajun food is hot and spicy, and Cajuns usually wash it down and cool it off with ice-cold beer. The meat is fresh off the farm. The seafood is right out of the Bayou. The spices are usually grown in the backyard. You would have to search hard to find a Cajun cook who uses anything prepackaged or canned.

Most Cajun recipes are passed along from generation to generation, rarely written down. If a Cajun is asked to give the recipe, it's usually given as, "a pinch of this or a dash of that"; most Cajun cooks blend spices together by eye, depending on their mood. Every recipe is open to change.

The base for many recipes is "roux," a blend of browned butter, flour, and oil, cooked until it reaches a honey color. Roux is used as a sauce mixture for all sorts of recipes from rice to crawfish to meat.

A favorite food is "dirty rice," cooked white rice with roux, chicken giblets, seasonings, and herbs. Dirty rice can be mixed in stuffings or eaten as a side dish. The recipes usually aren't given any more clearly than that, so mix and season to taste!

Here are some of the more popular recipes from different towns in the southern and southwestern Bayou. Experiment with them; welcome to the world of ad-lib Cajun cooking.

FIRST COURSES

GRAND ISLE CRAWFISH SALAD

3 cups boiled crawfish, peeled and diced
2 cups celery, chopped
4 hard-boiled eggs, chopped
1 scallion, chopped
2 tablespoons dill pickles, minced
5 green olives, chopped
4 tablespoons mayonnaise

Dash: salt, Tabasco sauce, pepper

Combine all ingredients in a large bowl. Add more mayonnaise to taste. Add salt and pepper and Tabasco sauce to taste, remembering the crawfish was salted when boiled.

Serves 4.

This salad is usually served as a side dish with lettuce or as a sandwich. Shrimp or crabmeat can be substituted for the crawfish.

ST. MARTINVILLE SHRIMP REMOULADE

Juice of 1 lemon
1 tablespoon hot mustard
2 tablespoons Tabasco sauce
5 tablespoons cooking oil
1 small onion, chopped
2 celery stalks, chopped
1½ pounds shrimp, peeled and cooked

Combine lemon juice, mustard, Tabasco sauce, and cooking oil. Heat until it begins to bubble slightly. Combine remaining ingredients and toss. Remove from heat. Let stand until it reaches room temperature, then refrigerate for at least 2½ hours. Stir before serving.

Serves 4.

Remoulade is a light salad that is usually served with fresh bread and strong Cajun coffee.

ABBEVILLE CRAB SOUP

1 quart creamy milk
2 tablespoons butter
2 hard-boiled eggs, diced
1 tablespoon flour
1 tablespoon Tabasco sauce
2 pounds crabmeat, chopped

Dash: pepper, lemon juice

Optional: 1 cup breadcrumbs

In a double boiler, add all ingredients except crabmeat and lemon. Stir over low heat until thick. Add crabmeat and simmer. Add lemon just before serving. Top with fresh breadcrumbs if desired.

Serves 8.

Cajuns love fresh seafood soup and serve it frequently as a light meal or with another entree. Shrimp can be substituted for the crab if desired.

NORCO CREAM OF CRAB SOUP

1 pound crabmeat
3 hard-boiled eggs
1 teaspoon salt
1 teaspoon dry mustard
1½ quarts milk, scalded
1 tablespoon butter
2 lemons, sliced

Dash: Tabasco sauce

Chop crabmeat and eggs and stir in seasonings. Add hot milk and cook in double boiler or over low heat. Add butter. Place lemon slices in soup tureen. Pour soup over slices.

Serves 6.

Cream of crab soup is served as an appetizer with supper, usually on Sunday, or can be eaten alone for a light afternoon meal.

OPELOUSAS CRAWFISH BISQUE

1 cup cooking oil
1 cup flour
1 large onion, chopped
1 celery stalk, chopped
1 small bell pepper, chopped
2 quarts boiling water
4 ounces crawfish fat
4 pounds peeled crawfish tails
6 hard-boiled eggs, peeled and sliced

Dash: salt, pepper, sugar, Tabasco sauce

Make a roux with oil and flour. Add onion, bell pepper, celery and sauté. Slowly add water and bring to a boil. Add salt, pepper, sugar, Tabasco sauce and crawfish fat. Cover and simmer for one hour. Add crawfish tails. Simmer for about 20 minutes. Serve with egg slices.

Serves 6 to 8.

Crawfish bisque is considered a Cajun soup and is eaten as a light meal or as one course in a meal.

MAIN DISHES

GOLDEN MEADOW ALLIGATOR STEAK

2 pounds alligator filet
½ cup Tabasco sauce
2 large onions, sliced
1 tablespoon thyme
1 fresh lemon, quartered
½ stick butter (4 tablespoons)

Dash: salt, pepper

Cut alligator into portion-size pieces and place on foil. Place foil in deep dish. Pour Tabasco sauce over alligator pieces. Add onion, salt, and pepper. Place in refrigerator for at least 1 hour. Remove. Add thyme and lemon. Put 1 pat of butter on each piece of alligator. Loosely cover with foil, and either barbecue in foil for 20 minutes or until done, or bake in foil and pan at 325° for 20 minutes or until tender.

Serves 6.

When barbecued, alligator steak becomes tender and juicy, especially when cooked in hot sauce and its own juices. The foil keeps these juices in the meat. Serve with plenty of beer or strong Cajun coffee.

RACELAND DEVILED CRABS

1 stick butter (8 tablespoons)
½ cup fresh breadcrumbs
1 tablespoon mayonnaise
1 pound crabmeat
¼ teaspoon hot mustard
1½ teaspoons Tabasco sauce
1 lemon, quartered

Dash: salt, pepper

Save: crab shells

Pour melted butter over breadcrumbs, mix with mayonnaise. Add crabmeat and mix gently. Spoon into shells; dot with hot mustard and Tabasco sauce. Bake at 350° for 30 minutes. Remove from oven and serve hot with lemon, salt, and pepper to taste.

Serves 4.

Deviled crabs are served at special occasions and special Sunday suppers. Serve them as a main dish with a seafood salad.

LAFOURCHE BOILED CRAWFISH

4 gallons of water
1 cup cooking oil
3 fresh lemon halves
3 large onions
26 ounces salt (1 box)
6 bay leaves
1 clove garlic, diced
1 tablespoon red pepper (cayenne)
1 pound yellow cornmeal
5 pounds per person whole crawfish

Boil water and add all ingredients except whole crawfish, cornmeal and half of the salt. Stir well until all the ingredients are mixed and salt is melted; cook slowly about 1 hour. While water is heating rinse and drain crawfish several times with ice-cold water. Mix cornmeal with remainder of salt and place crawfish in mixture. Set aside until water reaches rapid boil. When water is at a rapid boil, add only crawfish (without cornmeal mixture), keeping the water as hot as possible. Return to boil for about 1 minute; lower heat and simmer until tender. Remove from heat and drain. Sprinkle the remainder of salt on boiled crawfish if desired, and serve.

Boiled crawfish is probably the most popular food among the Cajuns. This recipe is used from the most elegant Bayou restaurants to the most casual piers along the Bayou edge. Just remember to serve with plenty of cold beer!

EVANGELINE STUFFED CRAWFISH HEADS

4 tablespoons cooking oil
1 small onion, chopped
2 celery stalks, chopped
1½ cloves garlic, minced
1 medium bell pepper, chopped
½ pound peeled crawfish tails
1 cup breadcrumbs
25–30 crawfish heads, cleaned

Dash: salt, red pepper, black pepper

Steam: 1½ cups white rice

In oil, sauté onion, celery, two-thirds of the garlic, and the bell pepper. Mince half of the crawfish tails with half of the breadcrumbs and add to sauté mixture. Add remainder of garlic and remainder of crawfish tails. Salt and pepper to taste. Simmer for 5 minutes. Cool to room temperature and stuff mixture into crawfish heads. Roll heads in remainder of breadcrumbs and bake at 375° for 20 minutes. Serve with steamed rice or add to crawfish bisque.

Serves 6.

Stuffed crawfish heads are probably the most unusual food found in the Bayou. The Cajuns are practical and don't like to waste anything. Considering an average portion of boiled crawfish is about 50 or so of the creatures, the Cajuns found themselves knee-deep in crawfish heads! Waste not, want not. Cajun ingenuity turned a pile of leftovers into a tasty recipe.

CROWLEY FRIED FROG LEGS

6 frog legs
1 cup wine vinegar
½ cup flour
1 stick butter (8 tablespoons)
¼ cup parsley, chopped
1 clove garlic, minced
½ cup sauterne wine, heated

Dash: salt, pepper, Tabasco sauce.

Marinate frog legs in wine vinegar in the refrigerator for at least 6 hours. Dry legs, then coat with flour, salt, and pepper. Melt butter. Add parsley, garlic, and Tabasco sauce. Add legs and cook over low heat, turning legs to cook through. When they are almost tender, add hot sauterne wine, barely covering bottom half of legs. Bring to a boil, then lower heat and let legs steam in wine. Baste until tender.

Serves 3.

Fried frog legs taste somewhat like sweet, tender chicken. Frog legs are plentiful in the Bayou, and frogging is a big business. Frog legs are reasonably priced in Louisiana, and not the expensive delicacy often found in eastern and midwestern restaurants.

CHAUVIN BAKED OYSTERS

1½ sticks melted butter (12 tablespoons)
3 cups fresh breadcrumbs
3 dozen fresh oysters, shucked
½ tablespoon Tabasco sauce

Save: oyster shells

Wash and dry 16 of the best oyster shells and put aside. Coat a deep baking dish with melted butter. Drain off excess, and cover bottom of the dish with some of the breadcrumbs. Dribble some of the excess butter over the breadcrumbs. Put a layer of oysters on top of the breadcrumbs. Add more breadcrumbs, sprinkle more butter, add more oysters in layers until the dish is filled or the oysters are used up. Bake at 375° for 15 to 20 minutes. Spoon the hot mixture into dry oyster shells. Sprinkle with lemon and Tabasco sauce.

Serves 4.

This recipe is a variation on Oysters Rockefeller, and can be a main dish for either lunch or dinner. It's easy to make and easy to serve.

MORGAN CITY OYSTER ROLLS

6 French bread rolls
1 pint oysters, shucked
3 tablespoons butter
2 tablespoons Tabasco sauce
Juice of ½ fresh lemon

Spoon out middle of rolls, so they form a shallow "boat." Over low heat, sauté oysters in butter and Tabasco sauce until they begin to curl slightly. Spoon into rolls and bake for 15 minutes at 375°. Remove from oven; squeeze lemon juice over filling.

Serves 6.

Oyster rolls are easy to prepare and can be served as a main dish with a salad.

GRAND CHENIER ROAST PIG

1 suckling pig, about 10 pounds, cleaned
dirty rice stuffing (see recipe page 57)
½ stick butter (4 tablespoons), melted
hot water
1 small red apple
2 cranberries

Dash: salt, pepper

Fill inside of pig loosely with dirty rice stuffing; sew securely, tie legs, and place pig in "kneeling" position in roasting pan. Baste with butter. Season with salt and pepper. Pour water in bottom of roasting pan. Roast at 350° for 3½ hours, basting frequently to keep skin from cracking. Remove from oven. Place on platter in same kneeling position. Insert cranberries for eyes and apple in mouth. Carve at right angles to backbone.

Serves 10.

Roast pig is associated with old Cajun "boucheries" or butcheries, where Cajun families would butcher a selected pig from their livestock and hold a feast with family, friends, and neighbors.

FRANKLIN DIRTY RICE AND BOUDIN

¾ pound boudin (see recipe below)
2 tablespoons hot water
1½ cups coarse breadcrumbs
1½ cups hot boiled rice
1½ cups chopped tomatoes and juice
¼ cup bell pepper, chopped
3 tablespoons celery, chopped
1½ tablespoons onion, chopped
2 tablespoons butter, in small pieces

Dash: salt, pepper

Cut boudin into small pieces and fry until brown. Add water. Combine breadcrumbs, rice, tomatoes and juice, pepper, celery, onion, and seasonings. Mix and add boudin. Spoon into greased casserole. Top with pieces of butter and bake at 375° for 30 minutes.

Serves 6.

Dirty rice and boudin is a popular dinner favorite; it is similar to some recipes for jambalaya with sausage.

RAYNE BOUDIN

10 cups water
1 cup parsley, chopped
1 cup celery, chopped
3 cups onion, chopped
½ bell pepper, chopped
4 pounds lean ground pork
2 pounds pork liver
4 cups cooked, white rice
3 teaspoons salt
2 teaspoons red pepper (cayenne)

Dollop: Tabasco sauce

Optional: sausage casings

Add to water all ingredients except rice, salt, pepper, and Tabasco. Bring to a boil, then stir and simmer for about an hour. Add more water if mixture begins to dry out. Remove from heat and let mixture cool to near room temperature. Add rice, salt, pepper, and Tabasco. Stir well. Either stuff mixture into sausage casings and simmer for an additional 10 minutes, or form patties and fry.

Serves: varies

Boudin is a staple in the Bayou. You'll find it as a course at everything from a midweek dinner to a "bons temps" Cajun wedding. It's one of the Cajuns' favorite ways to serve meat, and often the meat is fresh from a Cajun farm.

STEWS 'N' SUCH

BAYOU TECHE ALLIGATOR SAUCE PIQUANTE

3 pounds alligator meat
½ cup shortening
1¼ cups flour
3 large onions, chopped
1 large bell pepper, chopped
½ cup scallions, chopped
8 celery stalks, chopped
8 ounces tomato sauce
6 ounces tomato paste
1 tablespoon red pepper (cayenne)
1 cup water

Dollop: steak sauce, salt

Steam: 1½ cups white rice

Chop alligator meat into small strips, add steak sauce, and brown in a dash of shortening. Remove meat. Add the rest of the shortening and flour. Stir. Add onion, bell pepper, scallions, celery. Sauté slowly; add tomato sauce and paste. Stir. Add red pepper, water, and cook over medium heat for one-half hour. Stir and add alligator meat. Cook for one hour or until tender. Salt to taste. Serve over rice.

Serves 6.

Piquante is a hot sauce or dressing usually served over rice as a side or main dish. Any fowl or seafood can be substituted for alligator.

EUNICE CRAB ROYALE

3 tablespoons butter
3 tablespoons flour
⅔ cup cream
⅔ cup chicken stock
2 cups crabmeat, cooked
½ cup mushrooms, sliced
1 egg, beaten

Dash: salt, pepper

Steam: 1½ cups white rice

Make a roux of butter, flour, and seasonings. Slowly add liquid and stir constantly over low heat. Add crabmeat and mushrooms. Slowly add egg and stir until heated. Serve hot over steamed rice.

Serves 6.

Crab Royale is used as a side dish or a light meal. Serve with French bread.

BREAUX BRIDGE CRAWFISH ÉTOUFFÉE

1 large onion, sliced
1 small bell pepper, chopped
½ cup parsley, chopped
½ stick of butter (4 tablespoons)
¼ cup crawfish fat
1 tablespoon cornstarch mixed with ⅓ cup water
1 pound peeled crawfish

Dash: salt, pepper

Steam: ½ cup white rice

Sauté onions, bell pepper, and parsley in butter; add crawfish fat. Simmer for 20 minutes, turning occasionally. Slowly add salt, pepper, and cornstarch paste while stirring. Let mixture simmer. Slowly add peeled crawfish. Cover mixture and cook over medium heat for 10 minutes. Remove from heat and serve over steamed rice.

Serves 4.

Crawfish étouffée is a light fish stew with a delicate taste. It is served as a main dish.

HOUMA OYSTER JAMBALAYA

1 large onion, chopped
1 teaspoon red pepper (cayenne)
1 stick butter (8 tablespoons)
1 cup uncooked white rice
2 cups water
3 dozen oysters, cleaned and drained
1 tablespoon parsley, chopped

Dash: salt, pepper

Sauté onions and red pepper in butter until soft and brown. Add rice, pepper, salt, and water. Stir and simmer until rice is soft. Add oysters and simmer again until oysters are firm. Sprinkle with parsley and serve.

Serves 6.

There are many recipes for jambalaya, using fish, shrimp, oysters, sausage, or chicken. The basic recipe is the same, except the meat recipes use more spices and are hotter in taste. Jambalaya can be served as a main dish or a side dish.

LAFAYETTE RED BEANS AND RICE

2 tablespoons cooking oil
1 pound ground beef
1 large onion, chopped
1 medium bell pepper, chopped
1 pound whole tomatoes, undrained and chopped
1 cup water
1-pound can of red kidney beans

Dash: salt, pepper, Tabasco sauce, chili powder

Steam: 1½ cups white rice

Brown meat in oil and drain. Sauté onion and bell pepper with meat.
Add salt, pepper, chili powder, tomatoes, and water. Simmer 15 minutes over low heat. Add beans. Stir. Remove from heat and add
Tabasco sauce. Bake at 350° for 1 hour (make sure to cover tightly).
Remove from oven, stir in steamed rice. Leave covered for 15 minutes
to let juices blend.

Serves 6.

*Red beans and rice is a popular lunchtime meal, served with plenty of
extra hot sauce and cold beer.*

NEW IBERIA SEAFOOD GUMBO

10 tablespoons oil
10 tablespoons flour
1 cup onion, chopped
½ cup bell pepper, chopped
1 clove garlic, chopped
1 cup celery, chopped
8 ounces tomato sauce
1 pound peeled tomatoes, diced
1 cup oysters (reserve liquid)
2 quarts water
2 pounds peeled raw shrimp
1 cup crawfish meat
1 cup crab meat

Dash: pepper, Tabasco sauce

Steam: 1½ cups white rice

Make a roux with oil and flour. Over low heat, add onion, bell pepper, garlic, and celery. Sauté until tender. Add tomato sauce, peeled tomatoes, oyster liquid, and water. Simmer for 1 hour. Add shrimp, crawfish, oysters, and crabmeat. Cook over medium heat until shellfish is tender but firm. Season to taste. Serve in bowl over rice.

Serves 6.

There are scores of recipes for gumbo, some hot and spicy, others mild. Gumbo is basically a thick vegetable stew with meat. It can be made with any type of shellfish, fowl, or game.

PLAQUEMINE SEAFOOD STEW

1 large onion, chopped
1 clove garlic, chopped
2 celery stalks, chopped
3 cups hot water
3 tablespoons cooking oil
2 tablespoons flour
½ pint raw oysters
½ pound raw shrimp

Dash: salt, pepper, seasoning salt, Tabasco sauce

Steam: 1 cup white rice

Sauté onions and garlic in 1 tablespoon cooking oil. Add celery and water and simmer. In a separate saucepan, make a roux with remaining oil and flour, then add to simmering water. Add shellfish and seasonings to taste. Add more water if mixture begins to dry out. Simmer for 35 minutes, covered. Serve over rice.

Serves 4.

Cajuns make a stew out of just about anything, from oysters to crawfish, and even alligator. This recipe can be altered to accommodate other foods.

CUT OFF SHRIMP CREOLE

1 stick butter (8 tablespoons)
3 tablespoons flour
1 cup water
1 large onion, chopped
1 small bell pepper, chopped
½ teaspoon red pepper (cayenne)
½ teaspoon lemon juice
1 teaspoon brown sugar
8 ounces tomato sauce
2 pounds raw peeled shrimp

Dash: salt, pepper, Tabasco sauce

Steam: 1 cup white rice

To make a roux, add butter and flour to water. Melt over low heat and mix thoroughly. Add onion, bell pepper. Sauté mixture over medium heat. Add all other ingredients except shrimp, and simmer over low heat for 40 minutes, stirring occasionally. Add shrimp and cook until shrimp are tender. Serve over steamed rice.

Serves 6.

Shrimp Creole is a favorite in the Bayou, taken from the Louisiana Creole recipes and adapted to the Cajun way of cooking. It is served as a main dish.

MAMOU COUSH-COUSH

6 cups yellow cornmeal
2 teaspoons salt
2 tablespoons brown sugar
2 cups water
½ cup cooking oil

Mix cornmeal, salt, and sugar in large bowl, slowly adding water. Stir until mixed thoroughly. Heat cooking oil in deep frying pan. Add cornmeal mixture. Stir frequently to avoid lumping. Cook about 25 minutes or until cornmeal is golden brown. Serve hot with syrup or cold with milk.

Serves 6.

Coush-coush is a variation on an old Indian recipe. It is eaten with a meal in place of bread or as a snack or breakfast treat.

LAKE CHARLES PRALINES

4 cups brown sugar
2 cups milk
½ stick butter (4 tablespoons)
4 tablespoons corn syrup
½ teaspoon baking soda
2 teaspoons vanilla extract
3 cups chopped pecans or pecan halves

Mix all ingredients except pecans in a heavy saucepan. Boil and stir. Slowly add pecans, stirring while adding. Return mixture to a boil over medium heat. Stir rapidly until creamy. Spoon onto wax paper, foil, or a nonstick pan.

Makes 4 dozen.

Pralines are a popular sugary candy found throughout Louisiana and the South. It's more of a Southern tradition than Cajun, but enjoyed by Cajuns all the same.

The Cajun "bons temps" attitude is reflected in their cooking. Eating is more than just a routine habit or function—it's an event, a reason to get family and friends together to share stories and celebrate. Cajun food is a celebration and a tribute to a natural, fun-loving way of life.

Music and Dancing

"Pass a good time, cher! Laissez les bons temps rouler!"

A French accordian, fiddle, washboard, triangle ("ting-a-ling"), guitar, and a whole lot of people dancing, laughing, drinking, and raising a little hell. It's Saturday night at the *fais-dodo* (dance).

"When I die, don't send me to Heaven, Lord. Send me to La Poussière." It means "the dust," and that's what the Cajuns kick up, along with a good time, some deep-down laughs, and some free-spirited fun.

A Saturday night at a Cajun dance hall is a slice of heaven on earth. Troubles are left outside; there's not a somber face in the crowd. It's a smattering of Cajun-French, broken English, Southern slang, and mainstream American under one roof, in one massive riot of storytelling, gossip trading, joke swapping, dancing, and beer drinking, all to the tune of "ee-hee-hee," "aiyee," or "hey la bas!"

The music is simple, sweet, and joyous. It mixes the old Cajun-French lyrics with the new up-tempo beat, the old French accordian and washboard with steel guitars and drums. It's fast and lively, slow and quiet. It spins tales of sadness, of a love affair gone awry, of the evils of the world, of crime and punishment. But it also kicks up to a happy clip, proclaiming true love, prosperity, family, and a lovely old

65

inn deep in the Bayou. It is waltzes and jitterbugs, old people twirling around the floor with the young, balance and harmony, and just plain fun.

Cajun music is played on the downbeat, with sweet melodies and soulful chords. It's all played by ear, and passed from generation to generation on the knee of the grandfather to the grandson. One Cajun musician described Cajun music as "the heart and soul of what we're all about . . . fun, happy, sad. It's all there with a good-times beat. You can sit and listen to country. You either like it or you don't. But Cajun? Ah, my friend. Now that's real music. You can't sit still and listen to Cajun. If you're not out there dancing, you're here tapping your foot . . . and smiling. Find me one person here who ain't happy and having a good time." Cajun reflects the roots of the Bayou, and those who play Cajun play it because it's in their blood and their soul, not because it's popular or a way to earn a buck. Cajun hasn't been hyped or compromised the way country and western has. It's still pure and clean and takes you back some 200 years.

Cajun musicians are considered more or less the heroes of the Cajun people. They're the persons who are carrying on the tradition, leading the people out of their problems and into some fun. They're the bridge between the past and the present, reminding the Cajun people of their roots, yet popularizing the culture in the outside world. Next to authentic Cajun cooking and the Bayou swamps, perhaps nothing represents the Cajun people to the outside world better than their music. Cajun music on a Saturday night at a fais-dodo is a tradition that is far from dying in the culture. It has always been popular in the Bayou, and its popularity is spreading throughout the state of Louisiana and the South.

The Cajun music, as we know it today, has roots in early Acadian, French, Creole, Celtic, and Anglo-Saxon folk music. Many of the first Cajun songs were sung a cappella, backed up only with the clapping together of spoons, the "jang-jang" of a washboard, or the thumping and tapping of hands on a table or kitchen pot. Nothing was written down; most was composed as the musicians went along, using either poems about love affairs, families, and friends, or traditional tales about war, soldiers, or hardships—put to fragmented, off-the-cuff melodies. One person would pick up the words and music from the next, add a bit of his own style, and pass it along. Still others just pounded out beats and rhythms, composing tunes without lyrics per se—just shouts, cries, and Cajun expressions of happiness and joy. Cajuns used the music primarily as a way of releasing frustrations and hostilities either with themselves or the world. With Cajun music, anything goes, and no one was ever considered too loud or too loose. A good Cajun song or tune with a yell was always considered a lot better than coming to blows with a neighbor, and it helped maintain the Cajun attitude of "let the good times roll." The music eased a lot of pressure and burden in the early days, and gave the people a way to express all the hurt and despair they went through in their flight from Nova Scotia to Louisiana.

Cajun music has evolved slowly over the years, picking up in tempo, relying more on lyrics than simply the tune to carry the song. The instruments have also changed, becoming more standardized than the makeshift ones used by the early Cajuns. The fiddle, which was once the backbone of early Cajun bands, is almost entirely phased out, making way for electronic steel guitars and bass guitars.

The Cajun bands now center around the French accordion, which is nothing like the standard accordion you'll find at wedding receptions or Las Vegas hotel-lounge acts. The French accordion is smaller than a standard one; it looks more like a concertina. It is also played in a slightly different way. A standard accordion is more or less rolled from top to bottom as the sides are pushed together, or are only opened and closed halfway. The French accordion is lighter than the standard accordion, and there is a definite art and a bit of trickery involved in playing it. The Cajun-French accordion is literally a squeeze-box and is played as such. Cajun musicians push and pull the sides together, pumping, and ending up with some unusual high-pitched and seemingly off-key tones. Most Cajun musicians will tell you that it's not easy to learn unless you've grown up with a squeeze-box in your hands. Playing the French accordion is more than just hitting certain notes, too. The musicians say that if you don't really feel the music down deep in your soul, there's no faking it, and it will show.

If the French accordion is considered the bottom of the soul, another instrument is seen as the top of the soul, reaching all the way into the heavens. If you listen closely to Cajun music, you'll hear a sweet, ringing, bell-like sound piercing the background or pounding out the beat. The triangle, called the ting-a-ling, petit fer, or little iron, is a quiet but nonetheless important part of a Cajun band. It dates all the way back to the music's origins, and has maintained its place in the music. Along with the French accordion, it gives Cajun music a certain distinctive sound. No other music form steadily relies on the triangle as often as Cajun; it is played as an important instrument, not just a toy or additional piece of noise in the background. There's more to playing the triangle than hitting it. Cajun musicians strike it, tap it, and poke at it, all in different ways with varying degrees of strength to pull out a wide variety of sounds.

Cajun music is still evolving, and is not one standard sound throughout the Bayou. There are differences as you travel throughout the Gulf Coast region, with most of the differences being in the sounds of the instruments, as well as the instruments featured. Cajun bands in the rural parishes of Acadiana (Lafayette, Evangeline, Jefferson, Calcasieu, Vermilion, St. Landry, and Acadia) use the French accordion as the main instrument. Farther south in the Lafourche-Terrebonne Bayouland, the fiddle still takes center stage in some of the older bands, while steel guitars are dominating both the accordion and the fiddle. Cajuns consider the music more primitive and natural in the southern Bayou because it hasn't changed since it began in the region. Often you can tell the origin of a Cajun band by which instruments the band features. An accordion is a sure bet the band is from the more western areas; a fiddle means the southern regions.

Cajun music was jolted and pushed and influenced by other forms of music while it was still struggling to find its niche in the music world. That uncertain existence paralleled the uncertain lives of the Cajun people. The Cajuns never really felt strong outside pressure to conform to more standard ways of life and language until the 1920s, after World War I had improved methods of travel and brought greater exposure to different types of people. Prior to that time, the Bayou was looked upon as a remote area, almost nonexistent to the outside world. The people lived and worked in small, isolated communities, revolving around one another, almost completely self-sufficient. Then, suddenly, the Cajun people were shoved face to face with the outside world, and its influence began to carve its way into the Cajun culture. The Cajun-French language began to fade, making room for American English. Musicians in the cities most influenced by the outside, such as Lafayette, began using more conventional instruments. The music began to move away from lyrics about old Acadiana and the Acadian struggles, and gravitated toward songs about city life, city women, crime, jail, and struggles of more modern Cajuns. In the late 1920s jazz began to appear in Cajun music.

During the 1930s, southwestern Louisiana adapted to the New Orleans influence of hard jazz and swing. Cajuns picked up the tempo, played on the downbeat, and focused on more instrumentals. Hillbilly (before it was called country or country and western) was becoming popular in the South. Most hillbilly songs were sad and slow, with tales of woe and rough times. The country was in the midst of the Great Depression, and the Cajuns, though not hit as hard as most other people, identified with the hillbilly attitude of struggling—of poverty and not belonging. They added fiddles and a country sound to the music, still managing to blend with their culture, ending up with a unique sound that was neither Cajun nor country. That music was played alongside the older, classic Cajun-French music that was still loved throughout the Bayou.

This mixture of sounds, Cajun-country and Cajun-French, lasted until the beginning of the 1950s, when hard-core rock and roll swept the country. Cajun musicians found themselves far out of step with the rest of the country, and yet wanted to continue playing their own kind of music. The answer came in the form of rhythm and blues and in an old kind of black French music known as zydeco.

Zydeco, sung in French-Creole by black Cajuns in a raw, rhythm-and-blues style, is found primarily throughout southwestern Louisiana. The name is believed to be a creolized version of *les haricots* (snap beans), from the title of an old song, "L'Haricots sont pas salés" (the snap beans aren't salted). Zydeco music is a cousin to Cajun music. The primary division of the two forms is color, although that is now changing. Zydeco music focuses more on blues, and has themes ranging from love songs (like the Cajuns) to satire and ridicule (unlike the Cajuns). Early zydeco was mostly played at country dances and parties and took off into the mainstream when blacks began working in factories in nearby Texas and Mississippi.

Zydeco has continued to develop through the years, much as Cajun music has been affected in different ways by outside influences. Zydeco now uses the large piano accordion as its primary instrument, moving away from the smaller French accordion or guitar. The piano accordion offers musicians a great range of harmony and a full selection of scales. (Its scale is ascended in whole and half tones, whereas the Cajun accordion has buttons instead of keys, and its scale is limited to whole steps.)

The rub-board, or frottoir, is another key instrument in zydeco. It looks somewhat like a washboard and is played with a fork, metal rod, or metal thimbles. It gives a metallic scraping sound when played. It usually adds to the music, or keeps the beat much as the triangle does in Cajun music. Zydeco is also evolving into its own form, away from the Cajun influence, by using several other instruments usually not found in Cajun bands. Early zydeco bands used the fiddle, but since the heavy influence of rhythm and blues, which relies to a great extent on soulful saxophones, the zydeco musicians are gravitating toward saxophones and away from fiddles. As the final push away from classic Cajun, zydeco bands now have a full accompaniment of drums and electric guitars. Today, the only real similarities between Cajun and zydeco are that they are both centered in Louisiana, and they both play to the same style of dancing—the two-step and the waltz—with slight variations in the rhythm and dance steps.

The next big influence for the Bayou and its music came in the decade following the influx of rhythm and blues, rock and roll, and soul. The 1960s saw turbulent changes throughout the country, and those changes reached all the way to southern and southwestern Louisiana. Swamp-blues, as the style was called, was suddenly dated and old. The younger generation of Cajuns couldn't relate to that style of music, finding it removed from the original French-Cajun origins and out of step with the new rock movement. The Bayou saw the birth of yet another transition, a mixture of classic Cajun, blues, and rock. It was called swamp-pop, and helped to bridge the monumental gap between the music of the Cajuns and the music of the rest of America. Most of the swamp-pop artists scrambled for an identity and found a niche in country and western. Many Cajun musicians fled to Nashville and recorded country and middle-of-the-road hits for local bar and nightclub audiences—in effect, "selling out" in the panic.

The Cajun music might have been lost, or so adulterated that authentic Cajun would be impossible to find today, if it weren't for the older Cajun musicians who weathered the 1960s storm. Many felt they were too old or too established to adjust to the new swamp-pop style. Others never felt that affected by outside influences. Most older Cajun artists continued the classic Cajun style. They played at local Acadian bars and fais-dodos. They continued to record classic Cajun songs and tunes and made occasional radio and television appearances on local stations, keeping the roots alive. Cajun music also offered an outlet and escape for those who didn't like the new swamp-pop or didn't relate to the 1960s rock music. It was a time of festivals, such as Woodstock, and a growing trend to getting back to nature. For Cajuns, that meant large gatherings at outdoor Cajun music festivals, where the old had their chance to play alongside the newer forms of Cajun music. Getting back to nature also meant rediscovering roots, including classic Cajun music—accordion, ting-a-ling, and steel guitar or fiddle. The Cajuns' music was unique; it gave them a culture of their own when other forms of music seemed to blend into one big blur. The Cajun sound, once looked down on by both outsiders and the Cajun people, reestablished itself as a grassroots form of music that was strictly American in its development and style. Outsiders began to take a second look at Cajun music and found it something of a gentle escape from the hard-driving rock and roll. Slowly the trend shifted, and Cajun began to influence some forms of rock and roll. Soon popular rock artists were singing songs titled "Blue Bayou," "Born in the Bayou," and "Pork Salad Annie."

Today, two Cajun styles are emerging. One, holding its own, is the older, classic Cajun music. The other, which is venturing out of the Louisiana area, is a faster form of Cajun, using more guitars, drums, and the French accordion. This younger style is giving the country a chance to hear Cajun music, usually sung in French, in a style that doesn't sound foreign or old-fashioned. Most of the older musicians feel the turn to mass appeal is a good, progressive change that opens doors for them, too. No longer do they have to fight to keep Cajun music alive and try to adapt to the outside influences. Now outside influences are often adapting to and adopting the Cajun style or philosophy—or even just the feel of the Louisiana Bayou.

CODOFIL (the Council for the Development of French in Louisiana) has done a tremendous amount of work for Cajun music. The French language, and the music, had begun to die out in Louisiana, but CODOFIL has helped keep the French-Cajun spirit alive, and is making the younger Cajun musicians proud of their heritage by bringing in people from French Canada and France to help respark interest in French origins. CODOFIL conducts events such as its annual "Tribute to Cajun Music" to keep the momentum going.

The people of the region are also doing their part to keep Cajun alive. Music festivals are staged throughout the Bayou at various times of the year. Cajun record companies and Cajun dances are in just about every town. There are also Cajun radio shows—the most popular and publicized being Revon Reed's "Mamou Hour" (KEUN), broadcast live from Fred Tate's Lounge in Mamou every Saturday morning. Most of the radio shows are on weekends, with such hosts as Johnny Janot (KLVI in Beaumont), John Lloyd "Tee Bruce" Broussard (KPAC Port Arthur), Jerry Dugas (KJEF Jennings), Dudley Bernard (KLEB Golden Meadow), Leroy Martin (KTIB Thibodaux), Rod Rodrigue (KHOM Houma), Jim Soileau (KVPI Ville Platte), and Camay Doucet and Paul Marx (KSIG Crowley). Cajun music is also played on WYNK Baton Rouge, KSLO Opelousas, and KLCL Lake Charles. Television stations in cities such as Lafayette are beginning to broadcast Cajun-oriented music and dancing programs, running clips of old and new Cajun artists. Most of the radio and television shows are in French, but can be enjoyed by anyone who tunes in just to enjoy some real Cajun music. If there is any barrier, it could be the French-Cajun lyrics or talk between songs. Many Cajun musicians believe that barrier is more of a blessing than a hindrance, in that it kept outside influence to a minimum—it kept outsiders from tampering with the music or changing it drastically.

Authentic Cajun, the first music ever considered Cajun, with only a washboard, ting-a-ling, fiddle, or even just spoons banged on a tabletop, is all but dead in the Bayou. Today, Cajun music is electronic—electric guitars, bass, steel guitars, and microphones. It is what sells, and it is what the Cajun people want, although once in a while older Cajuns will look back and reminisce about the old days. Any rumblings are usually forgotten when the band starts up, electronics and all, and the dance floor fills with a lot of Cajuns raising a little ruckus on a Saturday night!

Fais-dodo; "go to sleep" is the literal translation, but Cajuns do anything but sleep at their dances. The tradition of the Cajun dances started in the 1800s, when Cajun bands consisted of nothing more than the men in the family picking some French songs on a squeezebox, ting-a-ling, and washboard. The family would invite only the relatives (which usually meant several generations of Cajuns numbering close to 100), and hold a dance in their home or yard. Those dances were called the *bal de maison* (dance or ball at home). The custom began spreading when Cajun families grew larger and larger with each generation marrying into other families, and the bals de maison grew too large for one home to accommodate the huge crowd of family members.

Dance halls began springing up in the Bayou around the turn of the century. Cajuns of all ages dressed in their finest clothes and headed to the hall for an evening of fun and dancing. In those early days, the entire family went to dance. Baby-sitters were unheard of, so while Mom and Dad two-stepped across the floor, the babies and young children were placed on chairs and told to go to sleep: *"Fais dodo."* Because everyone at the dance either was related or lived in the neighborhood, there were never any problems, fights, or disruptions, and everyone watched the children.

To an outsider, the Cajun bars and halls and fais-dodos can seem like a bit of Camelot in their charm, Disneyland in their magic, and old Paris in their romance. When you walk in, you notice the intimate atmosphere. Tables usually line the walls, hugging a wide-open dance floor. People are there to dance and let their hair down, not politely sit against the wall and engage in idle chatter. The lighting is comfortable—not too dark and not overly bright—and is conducive to friendly meetings and dancing.

The people who attend the dances dress up, but they don't dress to kill. The women are ladies; few wear pants, none wear jeans. The men are gentlemen; some wear suits, all are polished and pressed. The atmosphere is relaxed and friendly as people enter and find tables. There's no feeling of getting "picked up" or hustled, as there is in some bars outside the region. Most everyone knows everyone else in the hall. And they nod, smile, or give a friendly hello to new or unfamiliar faces. Outsiders are welcomed and included in the conversations, provided they can pick up a smattering of what's being said.

Some dance halls or bars have a slight cover charge, $2 or so. Once you get inside, there's no pressure to guzzle down beer or drinks. You're on your own to enjoy as you like. The owners have usually had the building in the family for years. It's considered the family business, and the family is looking to make a living, not a killing, off its customers/friends.

The Cajun band usually begins with a waltz, just to warm up the people and ease them into the mood. Most Cajuns wait a few minutes before casually sliding back their chairs and walking out with their partners. These dances are a ritual, and they're treated as such. If a man did not arrive with a woman, he will slowly work his way toward someone at another table, lean across the table, and ask her if she would care to dance. He will hold her chair, take her hand on his arm, and escort her to the floor. When the dance is over, he will escort her back to her table, hold her chair, and thank her. It's a dash of Southern charm and old-world etiquette that's seldom seen outside the Bayou.

Couples dance in two styles—the Cajun two-step and the Cajun waltz. (Some stouthearted do the jitterbug to really fast Cajun instrumentals, but usually only toward the end of the evening when everyone's loose and really bringing down the rafters. Then, every dance seems to end up in some sort of high-kicking jitterbug!)

The basic Cajun two-step has a "one, and two, and" rhythm. Step first with the right foot; bring the left foot to the right. Step forward again with the right foot and pause. Then repeat, starting with the left foot. The movement is step, close, step, and pause. This is the pattern for the man; the woman goes backward. The couple may dance cheek-to-cheek, taking small, close steps, or at arm's length, moving around the floor with larger, gliding steps—as if they were ice-skating.

The Cajun waltz is really any type of waltz that fits the music; fast or slow, just about any Cajun song will carry a waltz. The waltz is tricky at first, because it starts off on the left foot instead of the right. Step forward with the left foot, then sideways with the right; close the left foot toward the right foot, and take your weight off the left. Then step backward with the right in a rocking motion, sideways with the left, and close with the right going toward the left foot. Take your weight off the right foot in a rocking motion, and repeat. It sounds confusing at first, but is easily mastered with some practice.

As the evening wears on, inhibitions wear down. A few beers, a few laughs, a few dances, and the Cajuns really let loose. The old folks often put the young ones to shame when it comes to going wild and whooping it up. Ninety-year-old couples jump up and down in a lively Cajun two-step and literally hit the floor, swinging their arms, bobbing and twirling as if they were 20 again.

In the old days the dances would occasionally get out of hand, with one group asking for one song, another demanding another song, then almost coming to blows over whose song should be played first. The bands used to get pushed and shoved and caught in the middle, until halls began using a raised stage for their musicians. Trouble also arose when Cajun families got together at dances in private homes (bals de maison). Members of an opposing family would sometimes try to disrupt or even break up the evening dance. If the feud was strong, men would ride horseback into the dance, swinging bricks, clubs, sticks, and guns. They'd smash windows, shoot into the air, and break furniture, but rarely ever hurt anyone. More subtle disruptions included discreetly putting hot peppers into the waistbands of men's pants. The peppers would eventually slip through the pants and work their way to the dance floor where they would get crushed. The fumes would send dancers running out the door, coughing, choking, sneezing, gasping for fresh air. Another method was even more sneaky. The men would break into the dance and drop cuttings of horsehair on the dance floor. The dancers would glide across the floor, while the hair slowly worked its way up their legs, giving them a good, steady itch. Fortunately, that type of fun and games has died out in the Bayou. All the fun is had by celebrating with friends, not fighting with rival families. In fact, the unspoken house rule at all Cajun bars and dance halls is that all troubles and anger are left at the door. No one seems to mind the rule, and it's rarely broken.

Cajuns work all week for their evening of fun and are not quick to give it up because of a certain predesignated closing time. Some fais-dodos end because the band simply gets tired of playing. (Bands don't play "sets" with song after song, then a lengthy break. Instead, they usually play at a steady pace, relaxing for a short time between songs, allowing the dancers to take a breather before the next song.) Other dances end because the crowd has trickled down to a chosen few. Or it may be two or three in the morning, and the owners want to close up.

Cajun bars and dance halls are scattered throughout the southern and southwestern Bayou areas. Some alternate among Cajun, country, zydeco, and rock. Others focus only on good authentic Cajun, as classic Cajun is known today. Most of those dance halls attract an older crowd than the bars that rotate with rock. No matter what your age is, in a very short time you'll fit right in . . . and feel like one of the gang after a dance or two.

Here are a few places to help get your dreams started and turn you into a real foot-stomping Cajun!

Corner Bar, Breaux Bridge
Harry's Club, Breaux Bridge
Mulatte's Restaurant, Breaux Bridge
La Poussiere, Breaux Bridge
Whiskey River Club, Breaux Bridge
Carpet Room Lounge, Erath
Blue Goose Lounge, Eunice
Pat's Showboat Club, Henderson
Belvedere Club, Judice
Blue Angel, Lafayette
Grant Street Dance Hall, Lafayette
Lake Shore Club, Lake Arthur
Bamboo Club, Lake Charles

Step-Inn Club, Lawtell
Bourque's Club, Lewisberg
Fred Tate's Lounge, Mamou
Blue Moon Club, New Iberia
Slim's Y KiKi, Opelousas
Happy Landing, Pecaniere (St. Landry parish)
Cal's, Prairievelle
Clyde's Private Camp, Rayne
Town and Country Club, Riceville
Triangle Club, Scott
Snook's, Ville Platte

Cajun music is featured at many Cajun festivals; some festivals are even set up as showcases for various Cajun groups. Each year in Lafayette, the Festivals Acadiens are held in mid-September. Part of that celebration is called "The Cajun Music Festival," where more than a dozen Cajun bands play in Lafayette's Girard Park. Some 50,000 people turn out for that segment of the festival alone. Each music-oriented festival usually has a dance, or a local hall holds special dances in conjunction with the festival.

It's difficult to travel through the Bayou and come out without some exposure to Cajun music. Cajun records can be found at any record store in Louisiana. You'll hear Cajun music on the jukebox in any Cajun restaurant and some smaller Cajun stores. A flip around the car radio dial will usually land you on a station playing Cajun music in some form.

As you hear more and more Cajun music, you'll slowly be able to tell the various songs apart. (At first, many of them sound alike, especially if you don't speak French.) You'll probably be surprised to learn that some bands and songs have hit the national music charts, singing either country or swamp-pop, with few outsiders knowing they were Cajun bands or songs.

Here is a list of some of the popular Cajun bands, or musicians who have recorded songs about the Cajuns or the Bayou, along with some of their song titles.

Abshire, Nathan, and the Pine Grove Boys
"Games People Play"
"Musician's Life"
"Pine Grove Blues"
Anderson, Elton
"Secret of Love"
Ardion, Amadie
"Valse de Amities"
"Oberlin"

Badeaux and the Louisiana Aces
"The Back Door"
"Valse de Jolly Rogers"
"She Didn't Know I Was Married"
Balfa Brothers
"Family Waltz"
"Drunkard's Sorrow Waltz"
"Casses pas Ma Tete"
Barry, Joe
"I'm a Fool to Care"
Bergeron, Shirley
"J'ai Fait Mon Ede'e"
"French Rocking Boogie"
Bernard, Rod
"This Should Go On Forever"
Bonsall, Joe, and the Orange Playboys
"Step It Fast"
"Chickens Don't Lay"
"Hippy Ti-Yo"
"Chere Tout Tout"
Bopper, Big
"Chantilly Lace"
Bourque, Agnes
"La Vueve de Sept Ans"
Breaux, Amidie
"Hey Mom"
"Ma Blonde Est Partie"
Breaux, Pat and Gary
"The Road You Took"

Broussard, Alex
  "Le Sud de la Louisianne"
Broussard, Delton, and the Lawtell Playboys
  "Madeleine"
Broussard, Leroy
  "Lemonade Song"
Brown, Sidney, and the Traveler Playboys
  "Pestauche a Tante Nana"
Bruce, Vin
  "Dans la Louisianne"
  "Fille de la Ville"
  "Le Delaysay"
  "Jole Blon"

Cajun Trio
  "Pestauche a Tante Nana"
Carriere Brothers
  "La Robe a Parasol"
  "Blues a Bebe"
Charles, Bobby
  "See You Later Alligator"
Chavis, Boozoo
  "Paper in My Shoe"
Chenier, Clifton
  "Ay-Tete-Fee"
  "Louisiana Blues"
  "Oh! Lucille"
  "Tous les Temps en Temps"
Choates, Harry
  "Jole Blon"
  "Poor Hobo"
Clanton, Jimmy
  "Just a Dream"
Clark, Octa, and the Dixie Ramblers
  "La Valse des Meches"
  "Bosco Stomp"
Cookie and the Cupcakes
  "Mathilda"
  "Got You on My Mind"

Cormier, Lionel, and the Sundown Playboys
  "Cypress Inn Special"
Creedence Clearwater Revival
  "Born on the Bayou"
  "Pork Salad Annie"
Crochet, Cleveland
  "Sugar Bee"
  "Country Women"

Dale and Grace
  "I'm Leavin' It All Up to You"
  "Stop and Think It Over"
  "The Loneliest Night"
Doucet, Camay
  "Hold My False Teeth"
  "Mom I'm Still Your Little Boy"

Falcon, Joseph
  "Lafayette"
  "Fe Fe Ponchaux"
  "Ossun One-Step"
Fender, Freddy
  "Before the Next Teardrop Falls"
  "Wasted Days and Wasted Nights"
  "Secret Love"
Forestier, Blackie
  "99 Years Waltz"
  "Cajun Aces' Waltz"
Fred, John, and His Playboy Band
  "Judy in Disguise"
Fusilier, J. B.
  "Ma Chere Basett"

Garlow, Clarence
  "Bon Ton Roula"
Guidry, Doc
  "Chere Cherie"
  "The Little Fat Man"

Guillory, Chuck, and His Rhythm Boys
  "Tolan Waltz"

Hackberry Ramblers
  "Jole Blon"
  "Cajun Pogo"
Happy Fats
  "Les Veuve a Kita la Coulee"
  "Colinda"
Herbert, Adam, and the Country Playboys
  "My Turn Will Come"
Hulin, T. K.
  "I'm Not a Fool Anymore"

Jivin' Gene
  "Breaking Up Is Hard to Do"

Kershaw, Doug
  "Diggy Liggy Lo"
  "Hey Sheriff"
  "Louisiana Man"

Leblanc, Floyd
  "Over the Waves"
Lejune, Iry
  "Love Bridge Waltz"
  "Evangeline Special"
  "Calcasieu Waltz"
  "Teche Special"
Lightnin' Slim
  "Rooster Blues"
Lynn, Barbara
  "You'll Lose a Good Thing"

Matte, Bill
  "Parlez-Vous le Francais?"
Matte, Doris, and the Lake Charles Ramblers
  "She's Too Young to Marry"
  "Tracks of My Buggy"
McLain, Tommy
  "Sweet Dreams"

Newman, Jimmy
    "Cry, Cry Darling"
    "Lache pas la Patate"
    "Grin and Bear It"
    "Alligator Man"
    "Bayou Talk"
    "Louisiana Saturday Night"
    "Blue Lonely Winter"
    "Born to Love You"
    "Boo Dan"

Orbison, Roy
    "Blue Bayou"

Phillips, Phil
    "Sea of Love"

Pitre, Austin, and the Evangeline Playboys
    "Flumes dans Faires"
    "Opelousas Waltz"
    "Le Pauvre Hobo"

Preston, Johnny
    "Running Bear"

Rambling Aces
    "99 Years Waltz"
    "Musicians Waltz"

Richard, Belton, and His Musical Aces
    "For the Last Time"
    "Let the Cajuns Dance"
    "The Cajun Streak"

Roger, Aldus, and the Lafayette Playboys
    "Diga Ding Ding Dong"
    "Lafayette Playboys' Waltz"
    "Louisiana Waltz"
    "O.S.T. Special"

Ronstadt, Linda
    "Blue Bayou"

Slim Harpo
    "Rainin' in My Heart"
    "Baby Scratch My Back"
    "Tip On In"

Soileau, Leo
  "Mama Where You At?"
  "La Blues de Port Arthur"
Sonnier, Lee, and His Acadian Stars
  "War Widow Waltz"

Terry, Al
  "Watch Dog"
Thibodeaux, Geno
  "Teche Special"

Walker, Lawrence, and His Wandering Aces
  "Evangeline Waltz"
  "Walker Special"
  "Reno Waltz
Werner, Joe, and the Riverside Ramblers
  "Wondering"
West, Clint
  "Sweet Susannah"

This is by no means a complete list of every Cajun musician or Cajun-related song, but it does touch on some of the major artists or significant songs either from or about the Bayou.

Perhaps the two most famous Cajun musicians are Doug Kershaw and Clifton Chenier. Kershaw recorded in French and English and helped popularize Cajun by crossing over into country, appealing to the mass audience. Chenier is called the "King of Zydeco" and sounds a bit like a French Chuck Berry, with his fast, hard-driving, upbeat tempo.

New Cajun artists are continually emerging, making their mark in the music world in and out of the southern and southwestern Louisiana area. Some older Cajun musicians are afraid that the growing mass-market appeal of their music will water down the Cajun style and flavor. Most of the emerging Cajun musicians are relatively young, and grew up in the rock-and-roll age. Cajun music could become too electrified and show too much rock influence. Younger Cajuns, though, believe the transformation is healthy for the music. Although money isn't the primary goal of many of these musicians, they say mainstream acceptance will mean the possibility of earning a living solely as a Cajun musician. The market is wide open with little outside competition, and the music's novelty will draw crowds. In addition, attention will be focused on the Bayou and the Cajuns, spurring Cajuns on to be proud of their heritage and rediscover their French roots after years and generations of being ashamed of them.

There may be controversy between young and old Cajun musicians, but one fact remains: Cajun music is a very special gift, given to the rest of the world by a very special people.

Games and Recreation

CAJUNS HAVE SPECIAL ANIMALS, festivals, foods, and language, so it shouldn't be too surprising to learn that there are Cajun games. Games, especially card games, are very popular in the Bayou simply because it's easy to get a game going, get lots of friends involved, and—perhaps—walk away with a few hundred dollars in one evening. Cajuns love to win, and they'll usually bet on anyone or anything if there's the slightest chance of winning. They don't consider themselves real gamblers, though. Betting and cards are just two more ways of letting loose and having fun.

Playing cards is a big social tradition in southern and southwestern Louisiana. Often groups of women, men, or both will spend an evening playing cards, swapping gossip, and trading stories—and end up playing through the next morning. The big card nights are Saturday and Sunday, and Cajuns can spend entire weekends in a game of cards.

A Cajun card game moves fast, and the rules are always subject to change, depending on who brought the cards, who furnished the beer or food, or at whose house the game is being played. The rules can even change without notice, depending on who's taking a beating at the card table. Quite often, it's every man for himself, with everything up for grabs. Arguments do erupt; Cajuns will get close to slugging it out over who threw down the last ace or who won the last *bourrée*. Usually, though, just before the fighting gets serious, they'll have a good laugh, pour another beer, and get back to business. Most Cajuns—whatever the dispute was, or no matter how angry they get—forgive and forget in a matter of minutes. It's rare to find a Cajun who holds a grudge against a fellow Cajun or friend. They're serious about their games, but they also have the unusual ability to keep their perspective and attitude that "it's only a game," and they won't let a dispute ruin family relations or a good night's game of cards.

The most popular card game is called *bourrée*. It can be played with any number of people, but the more players, the more intense and interesting the game. Bourrée is somewhat like a cross between poker and bridge. Here's how you play:

Every player is dealt five cards, with the deal moving clockwise around the table. If the group is small, under five players, a "witter" is dealt. The witter is a dummy hand dealt to the table. Each player throws his ante in the middle of the table; the amount of the ante can vary according to the house rules. The dealer's last card is turned up; the suit of that card is trump. A player can throw down a maximum of three cards, drawing from the deck. If a player doesn't like any of his cards, he can ante up one more time and substitute his hand for the witter. The play then moves clockwise around the table, with every player laying down a card and taking tricks. If you can't play off the suit on the table, from the last player's turn, you try to play off the trump. The hands move quickly, with the highest card winning the particular hand. The person who wins the most hands wins the pot. (The number of hands to win is usually agreed before the start of the game.) Players who haven't won any hands during the game have to match the pot as the ante for the next round. (That's when the money goes and the game really heats up!) The winner only has to put in the regular ante to stay in the game or deal himself out of the next one.

That's the basic game of bourrée. Every card group has its own set of house rules and its own unusual twists and turns on the game. If one group gets together on a regular basis, they'll even post their own house rules when they play, making the kitchen look more like a gambling parlor than a home. One hand-painted sign tacked up on the kitchen wall posted the house rules for a version of bourrée:

1. You are forced up to the jack.
2. No talking in people's hand.
3. Head up savings only.
4. Card has to be covered to be bourrée.
5. If you renig, you are bourrée.
6. If head up with one trick made trump—play your ace then lead-off card.
7. One trick with ace, queen, jack, jack ace, or king.
8. If you are last player and play wrong, pick up and replay.

Only a real bourrée player would understand those rules—but only a real bourrée player would need to!

Another popular Cajun card game is called pedro. It's somewhat like bourrée, except the players play for points instead of the pot, and it's played more by women than men. It's a little slower than bourrée, and a bit closer to a standard bridge game.

Bourrée is considered a gambler's game, and pedro more of a social game usually played without money changing hands. Pedro is catching on in popularity, especially with Cajun teenagers who might not have a lot of money. It's not unusual to see a group of high schoolers getting up a game of pedro on the school grounds or in classrooms—hardly to the liking of local teachers!

Four people play pedro, in teams of two at a table. Each player is dealt nine cards, in sets of three, going three times around the table in a clockwise direction. The players look at their cards and bid on their hands. The high bid gets to name trump. Players throw away any cards they don't want and draw from the deck, to a maximum of six. (Three of the cards dealt are extra cards and are thrown into a pile.) The play begins when each player settles on six cards per hand, unless the player started off with more than six cards that are trump, in which case that player gets to keep the extra trump cards.

The ace, jack, ten, and deuce are all considered "up trump" and worth one point. The five, called the "pedro," is worth five points if it's in the same color as the trump (hearts and diamonds; spades and clubs). A player who holds the deuce will always win the point, no matter what the lead card is. A player can bid from six on up. If a player thinks he can take all the points, he can bid 14–28. (That means if a player fails to make the bid, he will lose 14 points. But if he makes all 14 points, he'll get 28—a double or nothing type of bet.) The house usually sets the point limit, often 52 or 104 points. Pedro games usually last through the night, but do have a definite end determined by the point limit, unlike bourrée, which has no definite quitting time.

Older Cajun men play euchre, which is a variation of bourrée. (In fact, euchre is one of scores of variations on bourrée found all over the Bayou.) It's played more like poker than standard bourrée, usually with higher stakes. The game is also a little slower than bourrée, with more cross-betting.

The socially oriented Cajuns plan entire evenings around visits with friends or relatives. A family may spend the whole day, or the afternoon, cooking Cajun food or snacks just to take along on their visit. Cajuns call their evening visits a *beillée* and say, "Let's make the beillée" when they're ready to pack the goodies, grab the children, and head out for another evening of friendly conversation or a cutthroat game of cards.

The family will usually go from house to house, stopping for a while at each house, collecting and trading stories, then swapping those stories at the next stop. This Cajun communication system keeps the whole town up on who is doing what, marrying whom, and working where. If the beillée goes late into the night (which it often does), the children may sleep over at the neighbor's house, while the older folks gather around the kitchen table, open the beer, grab the deck, and deal out a marathon game of bourrée, pedro, or euchre.

If the evenings are made for cards and socializing, then weekend afternoons are certainly made for horse racing. The major racetracks are in Ville Platte, Opelousas, Arnaudville, Couteau, Vinton, Mamou, and Lafayette. Racing is a highly profitable business for the local towns and for the state of Louisiana. For instance, Evangeline Downs in Lafayette cashed in nearly $50 million in bets in 1983, and paid out a record $2 million or so in state taxes. Unlike racetracks in other states, most of the Louisiana tracks are open all year, offering some of the best thoroughbred racing in the South. Clubhouses at the tracks offer a variety of drinks, fresh Gulf and Bayou seafood, and fresh Bayou game, with a good smattering of live Cajun music thrown in to get the high-rollers rolling. Not many eastern or western race tracks can compete with Cajun ones.

Racing at Cajun tracks is different from that at other tracks in the way the horses are actually run. A typical Cajun track is only 256 yards, compared with the average mile-long tracks (1760 yards) in major cities. The jockeys are very young when they start racing the Cajun thoroughbreds—some jockeys are as young as six years old—and race the same horse throughout its racing career. Cajuns claim their tracks offer the fastest horses and the youngest jockeys in the world. Few would dispute the age of the jockeys, but the claim on the horses might be another story because of what some Cajuns do at the smaller tracks.

Cajuns have an unusual outlook on racing and their horses. Outsiders would call it cheating. Cajuns just call it having an edge on the competition. One of the most common ways they get this edge is to falsify the birth records of the horses. A stable might register a horse born in October or September as having been born in January or February, knowing the four- or five-month age difference means a more mature and faster horse. The trick works in theory, but there's no way to tell if every other stable is also getting an edge by doing the same thing. Chances are the race is being run with the oldest colts in the business! That leaves the Cajun claim about having the world's fastest horses open to some dispute.

The Cajun theory of getting an edge doesn't stop at the stables. It goes all the way to the betting window and onto the racetrack itself. Cajuns officially bet in two ways: match bets and pool bets. Match bets are put up when the race or the odds are tied. For example, someone will bet that two horses will tie, or will bet against the odds to break a tie. (Cajuns don't believe in photo-finishes; close is good enough to declare a horse a winner.) Pool bets are made by friends or backers of the horses in the race, with all bets being equal and placed far in advance of the race. One person holds the pool bets, with each bettor's name listed in a book. Winners usually double their money in a pool bet. Incidentally, Cajun betting is strictly pay as you go; there are no bookies or IOUs.

That's the "legal" way to bet. There are also under-the-table bets on just about anything going on at the track—which horse will be first out of the gate, which horse will come in last; anything goes. Cajuns like to help the odds along, too, and will sometimes take part in questionable forms of getting an edge. Some Cajun jockeys use a small metal bar with blunt spikes in it to spur a horse along. Others put a similar device in the inside knee of their racing silks and give the horse a gentle poke in the ribs. Most of the young jockeys are discreet when they prod their horses, but won't deny having done it if asked. In fact, some quickly show off their little homemade devices almost as a badge of honor!

Even though outsiders consider this cheating, to Cajuns it's just evening up the odds. In Cajun philosophy, it's assumed that the other fellow is doing the same thing, or worse, so this just ensures a fair and even contest. It also follows the Cajun "bons temps" attitude that racing, and betting, is all in fun.

Cajuns take their betting seriously, but not the thing they're betting on. It's not unusual to see two Cajuns at the clubhouse in a full-blown argument over a bet or finish to a race, one really believing the other cheated him on his bet or switched the odds because of a bet. They'll be ready to slug it out right in the middle of the dance floor, but the music will start, tempers will cool, and soon the men will be laughing and swapping stories, arm in arm, at the clubhouse bar. All is quickly forgotten until the next bets are placed. And you'll probably find the argument wasn't over a bet on the thoroughbred race, but over a side bet on one of the hundreds of things Cajuns bet on.

There's an old Cajun joke that seems to sum up their attitude on betting and racing horses—the bets are serious, the race doesn't matter. It goes like this:

An old Cajun entered his eight-year-old horse in a race at a local track. It was the old horse's first race. No one knew much about the horse, so the odds were posted 20-to-1 against it. It ended up winning, leaving the rest of the pack in a cloud of dust. One Cajun who bet against the old horse was particularly angry about his heavy losses, and asked the owner why, if the horse was so fast, he never entered it in a race before. The old Cajun answered this way. "Well, mah fran, ah tell you. Ah had dees here hoss in a pasteer and it took us seven years to ketch 'im."

So much for Cajun philosophy.

Cajun Country is also the heart of cockfighting, a sport that was declared illegal years ago, but still goes on in many towns throughout the South. Local authorities often look the other way when some of the bigger cockfights are held. Cajun cockfights are more than just throwing two mean roosters into an arena and watching them peck the daylights out of each other. An entire underground industry is built around Cajun cockfights; there are special farms, training facilities, and elaborate cockfighting rings all through the Bayou. Fighting roosters are raised on chicken farms, next to other roosters and chickens, until they are mature. The roosters selected and trained for cockfighting are those that show aggressive, hostile tendencies when they're in with the other roosters and hens. Most fighting roosters are red and black, mainly because they look more aggressive and fierce than roosters of other colors.

Most of the rooster training facilities look more like miniature, makeshift gyms than henhouses. There are special runs for the roosters to build up their leg muscles. Walls have holes in them for the roosters to peck through to strengthen their necks and pecking reflexes. (A cup of food is placed on the other side of the hole.) Trainers toss the roosters in the air 100 times a day to get them used to flying and landing and to strengthen their wings. Trainers poke at the roosters, simulating attacks by other roosters, so they'll know how to defend themselves. The only thing missing from the rooster training facilities is a rooster sauna and whirlpool!

The cockfight arenas are small, with wooden benches stacked bleacher-style to the ceiling, in a circle. At the bottom and center of the circle is a large, open cage with a smooth floor. That's where the roosters fight and their owners stand to push the birds back together when they separate. The arenas are dark and stuffy with a heavy, sullen atmosphere, more or less fitting a place built solely to accommodate a sport that ends in blood and death.

When betting on the roosters, the bettor always bets with his friends if he doesn't have a personal stake in the fight. If a friend or relative has a rooster in the fight, he always bets with the rooster, no matter how small the chances are that the rooster will win. Betting against a friend is considered a disgrace, and the guilty Cajun could be ostracized.

Cockfighting is slowly dying out in the Bayou, partly because of its illegality, and partly because it's in such direct contrast to the Cajun life-style, where the people share the land with the animals.

Even though many Cajuns feel there is no better life than that in the Bayou, where people are friendly, the scenery is beautiful, and the climate is temperate, even Cajuns need to "get away from it all." When Cajuns get away, though, they don't go to big cities on expensive, elaborate, drive-as-fast-as-you-can vacations. Cajuns hide out and relax right in their own backyard—the deep, dark Bayou.

A family or group of friends pack only the bare necessities and paddle out in a pirogue. As they go deeper and deeper into the Bayou, they encounter alligators, huge snakes dripping from the moss-choked cypress trees, or swarms of mosquitoes—but they consider it fun. They'll usually go so far into the Bayou that the water becomes thick and green with algae. To get through the murky part of the swamps, they either have to wade through and pull the boat or push the boat across the swamp with a pole. (No Cajuns ever venture out into the Bayou without a strong pole. They use it not only to push the pirogue through, but also to club alligators or knock snakes out of trees.)

Most Cajuns camp in early summer or mid-fall, when the Bayou is cool and the rains have not yet begun. In summer, the Bayou can get so hot that temperatures in the mid-90s will turn the swamps into a steam chamber with little air circulation and swarms of hungry mosquitoes. In the fall, when the weather is clear and the temperature cooler, there's probably no place more beautiful than the Bayou. Off in the distance, you can see a faint campfire, hear the crackling of wood, and smell the sweet aroma of fresh fish sizzling over an open fire.

The Cajuns set up camps on remote little areas of dry land deep in the Bayou—places impossible to find without a Cajun guide. The Cajuns either pitch a tent or sleep under the stars on beds made of cypress moss. They live off nature, hunting or fishing for the day's food, cooking fresh crab or duck over an open fire.

Cajuns respect each other's camps. Once one Cajun has staked his claim, others honor that claim and won't set foot on the campground without permission. The Bayou is so expansive and bountiful that there's no need to crowd with others, anyway.

Whether it's through a friendly game of cards, an afternoon at the racetrack, or a weekend in the Bayou, Cajuns enjoy their time off, and make the most of it. Fun and good times in the Bayou: the Cajun way of life.

Crafts

IT'S A HOT, STEAMY AFTERNOON in the Bayou. Men and women in small pirogues slowly push their way through the thick, choking algae, deep into the Bayou around dead and rotting cypress trees. The long-hanging cypress branches are smothered in thick, brownish green moss. Mixed with the moss and barely noticeable are snakes, hanging and waiting to encircle themselves around a victim.

The Cajuns pole the pirogue near one of the trees. With the pole, they snap a snake out of the tree and fling it into the murky water. Then they slowly reach up and tug at the moss, pulling it from the cypress into the boat. They might climb the tree and chop long pieces off with an ax. Soon the boat is filled with moss, and the Cajuns carefully make their way back out of swamp, toward civilization, past alligators lying quietly, watching and waiting for one mistake.

Spanish moss is one of the eeriest things about the Bayou. When the moss is really thick, it almost looks like a shroud draped over the swamp, barely letting any light through. After it's been thinned, it looks more like lace gracefully hanging on the trees, fluttering in the breeze. It thrives in sunny, humid conditions and clings to stable, solid objects such as cypress or oak trees or telephone wires. The moss does not kill host trees, but can damage them during heavy rainstorms when it is water-logged and heavy. It propagates mainly through its branches. New branches take root and grow, or a bird will drop a broken branch, which will begin to root. The moss is a self-propagating, natural resource that's kept many Cajuns comfortable and given them a steady source of income in difficult times.

Many Cajuns still gather moss much the same way they did 200 or more years ago. Early Acadian settlers found the soft, durable moss ideal for stuffing mattresses and chairs and for weaving and decorations. The moss was woven while still wet, formed into harnesses, bridles, saddle blankets, and rope. Moss was also mixed with clay to form rugged bricks for building.

Moss gathering is still practiced by older Cajuns who have been using the free natural resource since childhood, when other materials were either unavailable or too expensive. Younger Cajuns are used to buying more conventional mattresses and cushions, so moss gathering is slowly dying out in the Bayou.

Several ginning mills are still in full operation in southwestern Louisiana. Cajuns gather the moss and stack it into large piles, much the same way farmers stack hay. As the top dries, they turn over the piles. When the moss is completely dry, they bundle it up and send it to mills in Plaquemine, St. Martinville, Mermentau, New Roads, Houma, Bunkie, Marrero, or Goudeau. Behind some Cajun homes, you'll still find large, one-room wood storage shacks, called bousillage cottages, used for processing the moss at home.

The Cajuns stuff mattresses with moss and stitch them up by hand. When the moss becomes matted or stale, it is extracted and put outdoors, where it is piled, raked, and fluffed. When the moss is again fresh, Cajuns stuff it back in the mattress and sew it in. Reusing the moss isn't without its hazards, as an old Cajun story testifies.

Two old Cajuns put their old mattress outside and shook out the moss to let it freshen in the air. After letting the moss spend a day in the clean Bayou air, the wife gathered it and stuffed it back in the old handmade mattress. That night, the two old Cajuns went to sleep. All of a sudden, the old man felt something shove him. He thought it was his wife and paid no mind. It shoved him again and again. He woke up madder than a muskrat. Before he could say anything, his wife woke up screaming because something bit her. When they got out of bed, they saw a bump moving around in the middle of the mattress. The old man pulled the mattress off the bed and ripped it open. Out popped a Bayou chicken, and it walked off happy as ever, back into the Bayou.

There are other stories and jokes about nutria and even alligators getting shoved into mattresses with the moss. Cajuns will be more than happy to tell you the stories, but they won't tell you if they really happened or not. To a Cajun, it doesn't really matter.

Cajuns find many uses for the moss, in addition to mattress and furniture stuffing and horse equipment. They braid, weave, twist, cut, and mat the dried moss into decorations and use them in all sorts of Cajun crafts. The dried moss can be dyed bright colors and used in Mardi Gras costumes. Many of the light, airy-looking strands hanging from floats, masks, and costumes are not feathers, but moss, picked and dyed by a deep-Bayou Cajun. Cajun crafts shows often feature dolls made of straw and moss, along with blankets and tapestries woven by hand with Bayou moss.

There's an old Cajun philosophy that if it can be done, it's better if it's made by hand. Many Cajuns still practice that philosophy and make quite a few of their household furnishings the old-fashioned way. Cajun men chop down cypress and oak trees from the Bayou, split the logs, saw and sand the lumber, and make their own tables, chairs, dressers, cabinets, and pegwood flooring. Each piece of furniture is unique and lasts for ages. Many of the historic Cajun mansions, plantations, and restored early Acadian houses are filled with handmade furniture that is more than 250 years old and still in terrific condition. An off-road tour through any of the towns in southern and southwestern Louisiana will probably turn up Cajun families that still make their own furniture, and might make some specialty furniture to sell.

Cajun crafts shows are held throughout the Bayou at various times of the year. In fact, some sort of major show or local crafts sale is held in just about any given week in some town. Cajun women bake special breads, cakes, and pies and sell homemade braided rugs, brooms, pottery, aprons, dolls, and knickknacks. The crafts are usually reasonably priced and have a real Southern-country feel to them. They're a way to bring a little of the Bayou home.

FOLKLORE

Cures and Remedies

H ER NAME IS WISTERIA, and she's as soft and gentle as the flower whose name she possesses. An old soul with a young heart, she makes the land and its people come alive with love. She's a magical, wonderful lady who opens her home to strangers, offers them a home-cooked meal of shrimp and rice, and turns the strangers into friends. She's the grandmother everyone wishes for— the fairy godmother who is always there to help.

Wisteria lives in a small, tattered, wood-frame house on the water's edge in the southern Bayou. Her address is simple: turn left after the bridge, then ask anyone where Wisteria's home is. Everyone, of course, knows. She has no formal address, just her name scribbled in blue paint on a rickety old mailbox above the numbers 687B.

Old wood steps lead to the front porch. All that separates the outside from the inside is a shaky, crooked, screen door held together by one hinge and some staples. Her front porch is crowded with bottles of fresh Bayou water that a friend brought as a gift. Just barely hanging on the wall are drawings by some of the scores of "adopted" children who come to visit.

Wisteria's home is small, really nothing more than one room subdivided into a bedroom, bathroom, living room, and kitchen. At first, it looks old and cluttered with religious statues and paintings, dolls, odds and ends, and childhood mementos.

Wisteria's home has none of the modern conveniences. Her only concession is an old iron floor heater barely chugging on, leaning against the wall in the corner of the living room. Instead of dwelling on how little she has, however, visitors in Wisteria's presence begin to realize how little the outside world really has because it lost the simplicity and gentleness that now seems so right and natural. Wisteria has worked her magic.

Wisteria's house is surrounded by strange and beautiful plants, trees, and flowers. But those plants are not there only for their beauty. Wisteria believes, as do most Cajuns, that all sickness comes from nature, and nature, in turn, will always provide the cure. Within Wisteria's garden lies the cure. She blends leaves, branches, bark, and roots together into teas or compresses—a different combination for each individual ailment. Cajuns come from miles around to regain their health. Wisteria turns no one away.

Most of the cures are based on folk medicine, with a good helping of common sense mixed in. The Cajuns make no promises with their cures, because once taken out of the Bayou, they lose two important ingredients—the magic of the Bayou and Wisteria's special loving touch.

Here are some of Wisteria's remedies, along with some other common Cajun folk cures, passed down through generations.

ARTHRITIS

Take one handful of elderberry leaves. Boil in one cup of water until the water turns green. Add two teaspoons of sugar or honey. Pour into a cup and sip.

One handful of peach-tree leaves, seared in water, then mashed into a paste, will ease stiffness when placed on the afflicted area.

ASTHMA

Three fresh radishes, squeezed and strained and applied to the tongue, will clear the lungs.

Sleep on a pillow of dried elderberry leaves to clear sinuses.

Steep the leaves of an aloe plant until the water becomes thick and greenish. Strain and sip the aloe water during the day.

Cut a licorice stick into small slices and steep in a small pot of water for about a day. Sip the mixture.

A spoonful of ground mustard seed mixed with honey is good to ease an asthmatic cough.

BEE STINGS OR INSECT BITES

An application of fresh honey will ease the pain of a bee sting and take out the redness and swelling.

Lemon juice, on a piece of cloth, will ease the pain of a sting.

Damp tea leaves, or the damp leaves from any plant, will ease hornet and wasp stings.

Lime water or bicarbonate of soda (baking soda) in a compress will reduce swelling.

Rub bee stings with garlic or onion, and pain will slowly go away.

BLOOD CLEANSERS

Any bitter tea will clean your blood; the more bitter, the more effective the cleansing will be.

Thornberry branches and berries, when boiled in a small pot of water, make an effective purifying tea.

BOILS

Sear a handful of corn husks until they become mushy. Apply the husks directly over the boil.

Boil elderberry leaves in shallow water until they form a green paste. Apply the paste to the boil overnight.

Halve an onion, scoop out the center, and place the "onion cup" over the boil for at least one hour.

Take the "skin" of a boiled egg white and place it over the boil. Change frequently.

BURNS

Cut a fresh leaf from an aloe plant. Open it and place the juicy part over burn.

Baking soda, mixed with a little water, should be applied to the burn as a compress.

Take a slice of fresh pumpkin and apply it directly to the wound.

Ice helps reduce the pain and swelling of more serious burns.

A handful of willow and daisy leaves in a cup of boiling water will ease the pain of burns when you apply the cooled liquid to the inflamed area.

COLDS AND COUGHS

Honey and quinine water, sipped slowly, will break a cough.

Take one handful of spearmint leaves, boil in water, and add honey. This tea will ease cold symptoms.

Mint leaves or horseradish, steeped in lukewarm water, will give off a pleasant, cleansing steam. Hold your head over the steam and inhale to clear cold stuffiness.

Inhale garlic vapors to clear the head.

Hot, steamed onions, used as a compress over the chest, will help break a cold.

Take a hot bath, and sip rum or brandy before going to sleep. The warmth from both will force out the cold.

CONSTIPATION AND DIARRHEA

Take a chunk of oak-tree bark and scrape off the inside. Boil the white scrapings in a cup of water and drink. This will stop diarrhea.

Raw apples or bananas will ease diarrhea, as will a teaspoon or so of fresh, thick cream.

Sip as often as possible hot lemonade or peppermint tea to stop diarrhea.

A spoonful of hot lemonade mixed with olive oil will stop constipation.

Blackstrap molasses will help constipation if taken at regular four-hour intervals.

Flush out the system with plenty of water, sipped throughout the day.

EARACHE

Drops of warm, fresh milk in the ear canal will ease pain.

Steep garlic in warm olive oil, and put the clove into the ear canal for several minutes.

EYESTRAIN

Take a cool washcloth, wring out, and place over the eyes for 10 minutes. Repeat as necessary.

Slice cucumbers and put fleshy part over the eyes and relax.

FATIGUE

Boiled belladonna (deadly nightshade) will pick you up and ease tension and fatigue.

Fast, sipping only fresh fruit juices for one day. You'll feel refreshed and vital the following day.

Honey or lemon juice acts as a quick revitalizer.

Blend a raw egg in orange juice and sip in the morning and right before bedtime.

FEVER

Slice raw onions and apply them to the soles of the feet. The onions will slowly draw out the fever.

Eat or drink fresh strawberry or raspberry juice, or boil the leaves from the plants into a strong tea.

Mash elderberry leaves and berries, then boil in water and honey. Sip the mixture throughout the day.

Boil the peels and leaves from a lemon tree, and drink either hot or with ice to cool a fever.

Rub peppermint leaves and oil on the forehead, chest, and throat. Repeat when aroma begins to fade.

HAY FEVER AND ALLERGIES

Pinching or rubbing the ears or the tip of the nose will stop a sneeze.

Slice a raw onion and put it in a glass of water. Remove the onion after several minutes, and drink the liquid.

Eat plenty of brown rice and honey to ease hay fever symptoms.

Spearmint or peppermint tea will help ease stuffy or runny nose and sneezing.

HICCUPS

Stick your tongue as far out of your mouth as possible and hold it there for a minute. The hiccups will stop.

Chew crushed ice, or fresh spearmint, elderberry, or peppermint leaves.

Take a spoonful of raw sugar or honey.

Inhale dust or powder or any substance that will make you sneeze. A good sneeze will usually force hiccups away.

NAUSEA

Drink weak chamomile or elderberry tea, made from fresh leaves and flowers if possible.

Chew mint leaves until they lose their taste, then spit them out.

Sip lime or lemon juice, or vinegar mixed with water.

SKIN RASHES AND SUNBURN

Cut a leaf from an aloe plant and apply fleshy part to the skin. This will take the redness and itch out of a rash. It is also good for any type of sunburn.

Drink plenty of elderberry tea to flush the system of toxins.

Apply crushed garlic cloves to the affected area, changing the cloves frequently.

Wash thoroughly with fresh water and baking soda to relieve itch and redness.

SORE THROAT

Gargle with fresh elderberry tea as hot as possible without burning the throat.

Mix salt and lemon juice and gargle.

Bathe tonsils or throat with vinegar or camphor oil.

Chew cloves of garlic until they turn to pulp.

WOUNDS

Fresh aloe applied to an old wound will promote healing.

For surface cuts and scrapes, cover ground charcoal with a rag. Apply it to the wound. The coal absorbs the fluid from the wound; the rag holds the charcoal in place so the wound will not become irritated.

Wash a cut with a mild mixture of baking soda and water.

The "skin" of a boiled egg, when placed over a cut, will promote healing.

Gather cobwebs, press together, and apply to cut to promote healing.

Wet tea leaves, when placed on a wound, will remove the infection and help the wound to heal.

Take a handful of peach-tree leaves, boil in a cup of water, then mash the leaves to a pulp. Place the hot leaves on the wound until they cool off.

Instead of looking to blame someone or something for their illnesses, the Cajuns look within, believing that they brought on their illness because they somehow tipped out of balance with nature. The natural remedies put them back in balance. The magic must work, because the Cajuns are very happy people, and they live to ripe old ages.

Cajuns also believe that all healing comes from God, and a cure is only possible if the patient believes in God. Cajun healers, or *traiteurs* (treaters), also use the old custom of laying on of hands, simply placing their hands on or above the injured or afflicted area. While doing this, they pray for healing. Part of the custom is that traiteurs never ask for money or thanks for their special powers. Instead, a gift is presented as a token of thanks and love. The gift is usually something small, and is either left on the table or presented at a later date.

Cajuns also have a set of rules for the passing of these special healing powers through the generations. They believe the gift is passed from father to daughter and from mother to son. If the gift of healing were to be passed through the same sex, such as mother to daughter, the special powers would be weakened and eventually lost.

Along with their healing powers, many Cajun traiteurs practice forms of white magic or white witchcraft. They mix potions of herbs, animal parts, and flowers, and will usually have a concoction for any illness, problem, or emotional strain or desire. They call their spells and potions *gris-gris*, and can put either a bad gris-gris or a good gris-gris on an outsider or visitor. A deep-Bayou traiteur can make a person fall in love, become self-confident, succeed in a venture, or make the person suffer hardship, pain, or severe depression. Several "voo-doo" shops in the Bayou and New Orleans specialize in Cajun potions and remedies. The remedies are not to be taken lightly, either. Most of the mixtures are centuries-old recipes that have been carefully tested, proved, and handed down through generations.

When you travel deep into the Bayou looking for Cajun cures, remedies, or potions, be careful and believe. You could be sitting in a kitchen, sipping some homemade Cajun brew, and find yourself falling madly in love . . . or stumbling under a bad Cajun spell. Beware, and never cross a Cajun traiteur. But a traiteur on your side is the best good-luck charm you'll ever find.

Jean Lafitte and
Other Ghosts

THERE'S GOLD IN THE BAYOU! Buried treasure left behind by bands of wandering, cutthroat pirates. Untold wealth awaits in the swamps. The Bayou's banks are dotted with huge treasure chests, spilling over with gold, silver, and priceless jewels. It's open season and there for the taking; just bend down and pick it up. There's gold in the Bayou!

Or so the stories go. Legend has it that pirate Jean Lafitte, along with other pirates and bands of marauders, fled to the southern part of Louisiana to escape the law. They docked their pirate ships in the bays of Bayou Lafourche, or near the swampy banks of the Mississippi. When they fled their ships, they carried their treasure with them deep into the Bayou. The treasure, stolen in high-seas battles or in looting sprees through cities, soon became heavy, and the pirates hid it in the thick Bayou vegetation or buried it in shallow holes in the soft, swampy banks, intending to return for their fortunes. They rarely returned. Most were killed in battles with the law or other pirates, or they got lost in the Bayou and were presumably eaten by alligators or other swamp creatures. The treasure troves remained, buried, idle, and waiting for someone to dig them up and uncover their fortunes.

The Bayou had supposedly been a popular hiding ground for pirates and outlaws starting in the early 1700s. Spanish pirates fled to the region when Louisiana was under the rule of Spain. English pirates swarmed to the Bayou during the frequent struggles between France and England when England was using the then-uncharted territory as a dumping ground for troublemakers. French pirates had hideouts deep in the Bayou Lafourche area, along the Mississippi River when New Orleans was a strong French city. Until the last 150 years or so, the Bayou had not really been settled and was still an open wilderness. The vegetation was thick and overgrown, leaving plenty of room to accommodate hundreds of pirates and their renegade crews.

There are stories of French and English soldiers stalking the pirates, working their way through the Bayou in hope of flushing out the pirates and uncovering their treasure. Most were reportedly killed either by the pirates or by the wild Bayou creatures. Those who survived were said to have turned greedy once they found the treasure, and remained in the area with the loot, becoming pirates themselves.

Cajuns tell stories of early Acadian settlers unearthing thousands of dollars in gold and silver while working their plantations along the Bayou. Plantations along the Mississippi River were supposedly the best places to uncover pirates' treasure chests. In the late 1800s and early 1900s, Cajun plantation owners were said to be digging up buried treasure almost routinely, becoming rich overnight. There are stories today that many of those old plantations, now deserted or destroyed, were built on buried treasure—that the master homes were built over the spot where a treasure chest was reportedly buried, and the plantation owner dug but never found the chest.

There are no official records of any treasure having been abandoned in the swamps of the Bayou. The stories may be nothing more than fabrications and tall tales, but every so often bits and pieces do turn up. A handful of gold coins was found in a plantation field in 1979. They were cleaned and polished, and were dated back to 1754. They totaled several thousand dollars in value, and sparked renewed interest in Bayou fortune hunting. When "treasures" are uncovered, they usually amount to no more than a trinket, a fragment of a cup or necklace, or a few gold coins. An actual buried treasure chest or a large amount of antique coins or jewels has never been reported or recorded in official documents. But, as any Cajun will tell you, just because someone didn't go announcing it to the world, doesn't mean it never happened. Cajuns are quiet when it comes to money, and most likely, if any treasure was found, it was kept in the family with only a few coins traded in for money when it was needed—which would account for reports of only a few coins found at any one time.

Romantic tales of buried treasure don't stop with the swampy banks of the Bayou. Those stories are only the beginning of the legends of wealth, pirates, and stolen treasure. When the pirates raided ships or looted towns, they fled to the Bayou, docking in the Gulf or in bay areas. They tried to hide their ships in inlets, out of view from other ships passing through the area—often ships seeking revenge for the pirates' vandalism and cutthroat looting. When the pirates fled into the Bayou, they took most valuables with them, leaving little on board the ships. As the crew disbanded, or were killed off, the ships were forgotten and eventually ravaged by weather or other incoming ships. They slowly sank to the bottom of the Gulf.

Over the years, bits and pieces of those sunken pirate ships have washed to shore. Pieces of dishes, furniture, buttons, and swords have been reported along the banks and shoreline. Cajuns and outsiders have tried to find some of those ships, and diving expeditions have been reported since the 1920s. Some are said to have seen the skeletons of sunken pirate ships, but the remains were in too poor shape to be raised. There are stories that some saw open treasure chests left in the ships, filled with gold, silver, and jewels, as if trying to lure divers into a certain underwater grave. Divers told tales of strange creatures guarding the treasures, or of the open treasure chests being there one minute, then disappearing as the divers approached.

Of all the stories of sunken pirate ships, perhaps the most common and most factually sound, is the legend of the treasure of pirate Jean Lafitte. Lafitte supposedly entered and left New Orleans through Lake Pontchartrain, which surrounds the city to the north (the lake has an eastern channel into Lake Borgne, which empties into the Gulf). It is said that when Lafitte abandoned his ship in the lake, it eventually rotted and sank, taking with it more than $1,725,000 in gold. Divers have been trying to locate the ship, but so far have had little luck. They have not been discouraged, though, because almost anyone who lives in the area and knows about the legend is firmly convinced the ship is in the lake along with a fortune in gold.

Jean Lafitte was born in Bayonne in southwestern France in about 1780. He fled to the West Indies after revolution broke out in France in 1789. When the revolution engulfed San Domingo, where Lafitte was living, he stowed away on a ship heading for the United States. It was on the ship that Lafitte, still a young boy, learned the skills of sailing, navigation, and day-to-day survival on the high seas. Landing in New Orleans, Lafitte became a blacksmith, carving out a modest living. Legend has it that a tall, dark stranger wandered into the shop and told Lafitte tales of untold excitement and wealth in the slave-trading business. Lafitte joined a band of stalwart slave smugglers known as the Baratarian Smugglers. He led the group on midnight raids, branching from slaves to stolen property. Lafitte primarily stole from the rich and the bureaucrats, and sold stolen items to the poor at reasonable prices, so he was harbored by many farmers and settlers, who felt he was more or less a hero. Lafitte became the commander in chief of the Baratarian Smugglers, and eventually commandeered a small fleet of ships, escaping prosecution.

The Baratarian Smugglers became self-proclaimed privateers, and staged countless raids on Spanish ships, slaughtering Spanish soldiers and crew members of any Spanish-aligned ship. (Many believe his hatred for the Spanish was sparked by the death of his wife. A Spanish privateer attacked Lafitte and his wife while they were in the West Indies, stealing their possessions and food—starving his wife and nearly killing Lafitte.) Soon Lafitte's brother, Pierre, arrived from France and fought at his brother's side.

Lafitte quickly became a sore spot to the French government and Louisiana officials, who were still on somewhat friendly terms with the Spanish government. Lafitte and his brother threatened the tenuous governmental relations, and officials came down hard on the pirates. French soldiers, on orders to capture or kill, clashed with Lafitte and his band of merrymakers, ending in a fierce bloodbath, with scores of soldiers murdered. Governor Claiborne of Louisiana put a bounty of $500 on Lafitte's head, believing that the poor who sheltered their pirate hero would jump at the easy money. Lafitte countered with a $15,000 reward for the capture of the governor, resulting in defiance of the law and a virtual standstill.

Lafitte's brother, Pierre, was captured by government soldiers in a late-night raid at the pirates' campgrounds, and thrown into a government prison, where he became seriously ill. The year was 1813, and tensions were again mounting between the United States and Britain, with Britain trying to seize control of the Gulf region and the Louisiana territory. Lafitte was reportedly drawn into the conflict when British soldiers, on orders from the British crown, asked Lafitte to join with their government in return for a near-fortune in gold. They believed Lafitte could open the many Louisiana waterways to the British, giving them a decisive edge and victory in battle. Lafitte stalled his reply, and risked a visit with the governor to show him the British offer. In that meeting, Lafitte offered his services to the United States government in return for immunity and the freedom of his brother. His offer was flatly refused.

The war raged on, with the British preparing their final assault on New Orleans. The fall of the city would mean certain victory for the British. General Andrew Jackson, leader of the U.S. troops in the region, led a ragtag group of fighters into the battle, but they quickly lost ground. The government had repeatedly rebuffed Lafitte's offer of help, but now found itself forced to accept or lose the war. Jackson, on behalf of the United States government, persuaded the governor to accept Lafitte's terms and his assistance in the fight; he commissioned Lafitte as captain of the United States fleet, with his band of pirates as commissioned officers. Lafitte closed off the channels and waterways to the British, and turned his fleet of pirate ships into battleships. Together Lafitte and Jackson repelled the British and inflicted heavy casualties on the enemy in the Battle of New Orleans—the last battle against the British in the hard-fought War of 1812.

Lafitte was considered a hero and was honored by the United States government as a patriot. He and his men were now free to enjoy their ill-gotten gains without reprisal from the government. Lafitte mixed with, and was openly accepted by, high New Orleans society. He was dashing and rich and acquired the reputation of a ladies' man and a bon vivant, adopting the dress and manners of a polished and refined gentleman. As a war hero, he was invited into Bayou mansions and plantations and was placed at the top of guest lists.

Lafitte entertained dignitaries and officials at various bars and restaurants throughout the Bayou and New Orleans. He is said to have socialized frequently in the French Quarter with members of Napoleon Bonaparte's army. Legend has it that the warriors would sit for hours discussing battle strategies and plans, their different escapades and victories, and their romantic conquests. Lafitte advised the men in both professional and personal matters, and reportedly donated quite a bit of money and treasure to Bonaparte's various battle campaigns.

Today, if you walk the streets of the French Quarter, you can see bronze plaques designating restaurants or buildings where the pirate leader shared dinner and drinks with Bonaparte's friends and soldiers in the early 1800s.

Lafitte supposedly stayed in southern and southeastern Louisiana for several years, wandering in and out of the Bayou. Apparently in constant fear of falling prey to bands of pirates and thieves looking for the alleged millions in gold he stole, Lafitte is believed to have buried most of his treasure in and around the Mississippi River region and in the bays of the Bayou Lafourche area. He is supposed to have scattered his treasure throughout the entire region, leaving no more than a few thousand dollars in any one place, to prevent one person or group from uncovering his treasure and stealing it all with one lucky find. Lafitte would sneak off in the middle of the night and weave a shifting path toward one cache, all the while dodging and ducking, throwing anyone off the path who might be following him. He would then take only a few hundred dollars and rebury the rest, never carrying too much money at one time.

As Lafitte traveled through the Bayou, he would stop in certain towns or plantations for weeks at a time. He often stayed with Cajun plantation owners or farmers because he felt they would not betray him for his hidden treasure. He would give money to those who were in financial trouble, fund any number of political causes or campaigns in the Bayou, and open stores and restaurants. Sprinkled throughout the Bayou are old wooden buildings and shops named after Jean Lafitte, most located between New Orleans and Baton Rouge, and along the Mississippi River toward Donaldsonville and the Atchafalaya River.

From here, the legend of Jean Lafitte takes several turns. Some say Lafitte grew weary of the routine life of a regular citizen in New Orleans and just wandered out of the Bayou one day. Bored with his life, he eventually landed in Missouri, where he adopted a new name and life-style to escape his past notoriety. He is believed to have married again, settled down, raised a family, and died in obscurity at a ripe old age.

Others say he left the Bayou, lured back to the adventure and thrill of a pirate's life on the high seas. He supposedly went back to pillaging and looting, taking over what came to be known as Galveston, Texas, establishing a new group of cutthroat pirates, eventually running at odds with several governments because of his constant looting of trade ships in the Gulf. Some believe he was eventually killed, and was buried in Galveston in a simple grave, without fanfare, considered an outlaw and a killer in his last years.

History records his adventures in Texas and alliance with the Mexican government. (He supposedly supported the Mexican government in the struggle for control over Texas because it was the only government that backed his pirating off the Texas coast. The U.S., French, and Spanish governments were against Lafitte because he raided their ships as they came into port. Mexico was connected to the region by land and had no ships passing through the port. The Mexican government also enjoyed the disrupting influence Lafitte and his men had on the other countries' ships.)

Many Cajuns say that Lafitte was eventually driven from Galveston and returned to his friends and treasure in the Bayou. There, they say, he remained in hiding for several years, making the U.S. government believe he had been killed and buried in Texas. He resumed his life as a gentleman and a wandering jack-of-all-trades, moving from town to town along the Mississippi River, revealing his true identity to only a few close, trusted friends, deserting the million dollars in gold scattered all over the Bayou. They believe Lafitte abandoned the treasure when he turned his back on his former life-style.

And here the saga of Jean Lafitte ends. No one seems to know whatever became of Lafitte, or what name he adopted when he returned to the Bayou. They believe he spent a great deal of time at the plantation of Louis Arceneaux outside of Lafayette. (Arceneaux was the "Gabriel" of Longfellow's poem, *Evangeline,* about two ill-fated Acadian lovers.) Legend has it that Lafitte had buried a great deal of his pirate treasure somewhere on the plantation, but so far none has ever been found on the property.

The mystery of the last years of Jean Lafitte's life adds to the lure and romance of Lafitte's legend, making him a sort of romantic hero in the Bayou. Probably because of that romance, a legend has spread throughout the Bayou and New Orleans . . . a legend that hundreds of people, Cajuns and non-Cajuns alike, wholeheartedly confirm—the legend of the ghost of Jean Lafitte.

There are reports that Lafitte wanders the Bayou late at night, searching for his buried treasure. Some have seen a tall, slender, elegantly dressed pirate kneeling beside the water's edge, appearing to be digging, but no dirt ever moves. The ghost flickers and weaves in and out of sight for several minutes, then slowly fades away after it stops digging, as if it could not find the fortune it sought.

Others report sightings of Lafitte standing proudly near the Gulf, gazing out toward the water with his hand on his sword, looking as if he were ready to board his pirate ship and sail out for more adventure and looting. They say the ghost of Lafitte appears for only a moment or two, then slowly raises its sword and fades away.

The ghost of Jean Lafitte has also been sighted in New Orleans, lurking on street corners when tourists have gone home or to their hotels, and the people remaining are residents who know the legend of Jean Lafitte. They believe Lafitte feels at ease only with local French Quarter residents and will only appear for them, usually in the twilight hours just before the sun sets when the French Quarter has an eerie sort of light to it.

Sightings have been reported in several plantations and New Orleans–area antebellum mansions. People say they see a flash of light, then feel a strong draft. The lights flicker and the room becomes cold. Then, very slowly, the slender figure of a man comes into view. The ghostly figure may appear on a winding staircase or in a drawing room. The ghost walks up the stairs, stops, then fades away. In the drawing room, it walks toward a window, pauses, turns as if expecting someone, and when not finding that person, slowly vanishes. The lights flicker again and slowly return to normal. Some believe that Lafitte is searching for one of his loves; others believe the ghost is confused, has not accepted its death, and is looking for friends or familiar surroundings.

Some clairvoyant types of spiritual groups have tried to raise the ghost of Jean Lafitte on command. Others have been trying to communicate with the ghost in hopes of learning where Lafitte buried his treasure. To date, neither group has been successful. The sightings in the homes, although reported by many people at one sitting, have yet to be confirmed by those who are considered authorities on apparitions and the pirate. This nonconfirmation, of course, sparks stories that Lafitte is a clever ghost and will not appear before experts, maintaining his independence and remaining in complete control over the situation. They say Lafitte was a free-spirited renegade when he was alive and remains so in death. All this, they say, confirms the fact that the sightings are of Jean Lafitte.

People who have seen the ghost several times say they can pick up its feelings. Some claim the ghost of Lafitte is sad and confused, almost as if it were looking back on a life of looting and murder with sorrow and remorse, and frustrated because it can do nothing to right the wrong. They believe that Lafitte's punishment (whether self-imposed or decreed by a higher authority) is to wander for all time, never finding peace, never being allowed to reap the rewards of ill-gotten treasure. Others report the ghost as calm and peaceful, merely standing watch over its former stomping grounds. They believe the ghost appears simply to let the physical world know it is still around and guarding its gold and its favorite area—the Bayou.

One day, someone may learn the truth about the ghost, and find out if these sightings are simply the overactive imaginations of different people looking to add a bit of romance to the area and excitement to their lives. The sightings may be swamp gas given off by the thick vegetation, as is often the case with UFOs, turned into the dashing ghost by people whose eyes play tricks on them. The sightings could be hundreds of different ghosts of soldiers and pirates believed still haunting the Bayou and New Orleans, all unjustly labeled as the renegade pirate. Or it could be the ghost of Jean Lafitte, as almost all who have seen it will attest.

Cajuns tell many stories of apparitions of pirates and slain soldiers stalking the Bayou, fighting battles, searching for lost treasure. People who live along the banks of the Mississippi River say that quite often, when the Bayou is quiet, they'll see a faint, ghostly shadow of a pirate standing and watching, waiting for his ship or crew to return. Others report pirates standing near the bank, hovering over a faint shadow of a treasure chest, trying to lure them toward the chest. Some have actually gone to investigate the sightings and say they have found gold coins or pieces of a pirate's sword or costume on the site.

Just as unusual as the sightings of pirate ghosts are reports of pirate ships. Cajuns who live along the Bayou Lafourche bay areas, along the Gulf of Mexico, and at the Mississippi River waterways report the nighttime silence of a summer's evening being disrupted by a faint blast that sounds like a cannon or shotgun off in the distance. The noise could be a hunter, a log breaking, or any number of noises. But Cajuns believe it is a pirate's cannon firing on an enemy ship in the Bayou, or a gun duel or shootout between two pirates, fighting for stolen treasure deep in the Bayou. Hearing the blasts, the Cajuns usually just nod, and know. They are convinced of their belief because, they say, no hunters would venture out in the Bayou at night, and no sound rings with an eerie echo like a gun blast.

Others say they actually see battles off in the distance, through a cloud of smoke, appearing almost like a dream—except the dream is witnessed by several people at the same time. A cloud will begin to swirl out in the middle of the bay. As it becomes thicker and thicker, two ships slowly begin to form, almost as if they took shape out of the dust, coming from nowhere. As the ships form, one fires a cannon at the other. The smell of gunpowder drifts a short distance and can actually be smelled by people watching the pirate ships. After the shot, the cloud begins to swirl again, and slowly wraps around the ships, taking them with it as it dissipates. The air becomes still again, and the Bayou returns to normal.

The Cajuns say these two apparitions (hearing the blast and seeing the ships) have one thing in common. About a minute or two before they appear, or before the blast rings out, the Bayou suddenly grows still. The animals become quiet—no late-night chirping, no animals splashing in the water, no owls hooting or dogs howling. The wind also dies down completely, leaving the immediate area in an eerie vacuum of stillness. A second or two later, the cloud forms or the blast rings out. The animals screech or run in a panic, and the Bayou fills with the sound of animals, then slowly returns to the peace of a typical evening.

Some believe that sudden "quiet" is a natural phenomenon in the Bayou—or near any body of water. Air currents often shift in the night, creating a swirling motion when the temperature of the water meets the temperature of the air. A cloud of swamp gas gets caught in the middle of the changing air current, giving the appearance of a thick, swirling cloud.

As for the sightings of pirate ships? Again, some attribute them to nothing more than overactive imaginations of people peering into the normal swirling gas, finding a thick area or two, and deciding it looks like a pirate ship. One person tells the story to a neighbor, who decides he wants to see the ghost ships, too, and not be left out—only he embellishes his story a bit and passes it along until it becomes another legend.

Those who live in the Bayou say too many people have seen the pirates and the ships to dismiss them so easily. Too many strange occurrences have happened in connection with the sightings to call them nothing more than active imaginations.

One Cajun woman in Port Sulphur, in the southeastern tip of the Bayou, says the ghost of a pirate saved her life, the lives of her children, and their home by appearing to her one night. She says she felt the bedroom grow very damp and cold. The dark, shadowy figure of a man in a white shirt, brownish pants, and boots appeared in the corner of her room. She could not see the ghost's face, but claims the pirate ghost spoke to her. (She says the ghost didn't actually say anything aloud, but spoke to her as a voice in her mind, the way we talk to ourselves silently from time to time.) She was planning on going visiting the following night and was taking her children with her. But the pirate ghost told her not to travel, to stay inside her house. The next morning she made her apologies to her friends and stayed indoors the entire day. That evening, a fierce storm came up from the Gulf, completely unexpectedly. It uprooted trees, broke windows, and knocked down sheds. It even washed out one of the narrow roads just outside of town. She says she probably would have been killed because she would have been caught in that storm. The pirate ghost saved her life.

Other Cajuns tell similar stories of being warned of floods, danger, and even death by the ghosts of pirates. Others tell of pirates appearing to them in the middle of the night, warning them against an upcoming marriage, or about not trusting an outsider in a business deal. They claim the ghosts have given them information about the future that was impossible to know (inside information about drilling for oil or that certain wells will go dry), and warned them about future events that would have led to disaster (accidents that were near-misses and could have been fatal had someone stood in a certain location).

Besides pirates, other spirits are reportedly seen in the Bayou and New Orleans areas. Spirits of soldiers who were killed in the Battle of New Orleans, the Revolutionary War, or the Civil War are said to wander the region, looking to return home to their families. These ghosts appear to just about anyone who visits the area and stays for any length of time, unlike the pirate ghosts who usually appear only to Cajun residents of the Bayou and New Orleans areas. The soldiers are seen walking through the Bayou, off in the distance, or Cajuns hear a slow knocking at the front door, only to find no one there when they open the door.

Stories are told of ghosts, ghostly occurrences, and frightening apparitions in many antebellum mansions. Some of the plantations along the banks of the Mississippi River were abandoned after the Civil War or shortly after the turn of the century when they were sold to large corporations. The mansions are believed to be haunted by the former owners, and many have frightening tales of death and sorrow.

One mansion along the Mississippi River, just west of New Orleans, is a popular home for ghost hunters because it is said to hold the spirit of the woman who lived in the house in its heyday. She has been seen, dressed in a long, formal ball gown, walking through the mansion, appearing in doorways and corners. She is considered a harmless and friendly ghost—she does nothing more than appear in the night. That isn't true of all ghosts that haunt the Bayou-area plantations.

In one mansion, the rooms fill with the eerie echoes of a baby's cry. The cry slowly swells, becoming loud and almost deafening; it fades and again becomes louder. In another mansion a young mother gave birth to a baby girl out of wedlock. In her shame, she buried the baby alive in a living-room wall. People who have been in the mansion say they can hear the baby breathing in the wall. They claim any picture hung on that wall will be found smashed on the floor the next morning. In yet another mansion, a young child was killed in a carriage accident. His parents sealed off his room and never reopened it. When visitors now spend an evening in the house, they find the furniture impossible to rearrange. They say any attempts to move the furniture will be in vain; by morning they'll find it all put back the way it was when the child died.

There is talk of being possessed by some of these wandering ghosts, and there are legends of Cajuns eventually becoming the actual person who died many years before. The possessed person may take on the physical characteristics of the dead, adopting their mannerisms and old speech patterns—and sometimes even their memory. Someone who knew the deceased person, through stories, pictures, or an old memory, may even recognize the possessed person. Cajuns claim possession can only happen if the person actually wills it to happen. They believe a person cannot be possessed unless he or she wills it and denies God.

The Cajuns are strongly religious and generally devoutly Catholic, which seems a contradiction with their firm belief in ghosts and apparitions. Somehow, they're able to separate the two, saying that what they believe has little to do with what they actually see. They can't deny either, and instead of fighting the ghosts of the Bayou, they accept what they see as fact. (Few Cajuns accept the explanations of swamp gas and imagination.) Cajuns even say their belief in the ghosts is religious, in that they were sent by God either as messengers to warn them of danger as examples of God's punishment, so that Cajuns who are still alive can plainly see what a life of evil will mean after they die and are forced to wander for all eternity, never finding peace. Being forever without peace and happiness is considered the worst punishment that can be inflicted on a Cajun.

The stories of strange ghosts, eerie plantation mansions, dashing pirates, and buried treasure are all part of the mystery of the Bayou. The Bayou is filled with backwoods white magic and voodoo, which might be the reason these wandering spirits feel comfortable in the area. As we move toward the twenty-first century, many old superstitions and beliefs have been lost or dispelled. But in Louisiana, these legends gain recognition and respect as more and more people claim they saw or felt some of these strange apparitions in the Bayou. The Bayou is one of the last places in the United States where supernatural occurrences are reported with regularity.

For those who don't believe in ghosts, buried treasure, and magic, the Cajuns have one answer. They ask you to explain how some people were able to find gold coins, dating back to the mid-1700s, right on the spot where an apparition of a pirate appeared and pointed the way. They say you don't have to believe in the ghost if you don't want to—but try to explain away the gold coins.

Good luck, and don't be surprised if, when walking along the water's edge some evening when the moon is bright and the air is still, you see a flash of a tall, dashing stranger as you look over your shoulder. You stop suddenly, turn, and peer into the twilight. But there's no one there. Or is there?

Superstitions and Customs

Lurking deep in the Bayou is a creature that is half man–half beast. It howls in the night, roaming the Bayou looking for fresh raw flesh, whether human or animal. It's a cursed, wretched soul—a soul in misery with no God and no purpose except to wander in agony. It has sharp claws and sharp teeth, with the face and hands of a wolf. It snarls and grunts and foams at the mouth. It lurks, watching and waiting to tear the flesh from its victim's bones.

The curse of the loup-garou—the werewolf. Older Cajuns believe werewolves really exist and haunt the Bayou late at night. Many insist they've seen them, or know someone who has turned into a loup-garou. Younger Cajuns know of the legends, but never say if they believe or not, wanting to leave some room for doubt . . . just in case they're real. Cajuns say if you venture out into the Bayou alone late at night, you can hear the faint howl of the loups-garous as they search for victims or attack each other in a vain attempt to die and end their misery. Loups-garous can never kill themselves. And they're not easy to kill.

The legend of the loup-garou began when the Acadians first settled in southern Louisiana. They came to a strange area with all kinds of

120

weird and unusual creatures. The legend of werewolves had been known for centuries, and the Acadians carried many of their old-world legends with them. Some Cajuns say there really were wolves in the Bayou that frightened the early settlers. Others believe the werewolves were black bears, which wandered the Bayou in abundance in the late 1700s. Others claim it was nothing more than Spanish moss swaying in the wind. But those who insist they really know will tell you the howling was real, and the werewolves really did—and still do—exist. Loups-garous are the most dreaded and feared of all Bayou legends because of the uncertainty of their existence.

You become a loup-garou in two ways—you can get bitten by another loup-garou, or you can disavow God and religion and will the evil on yourself. The first is the most feared by Cajuns because they never know where the loup-garou is or when it will strike. It can attack you at night when it crawls out of the Bayou, and either kill you or (worse) suck your blood and turn you into a loup-garou so you will wander the Bayou for eternity.

Older Cajuns say the loups-garous rub themselves with some sort of voodoo grease so they shine in the night. They also say they hold evil, mysterious dances in the full moon, all huddled together around a fire, howling and baying in the moonlight. They meet in an area called Bayou Goula and dance, perform black magic, and chant curses, much like a witches' coven. They chant to Satan and other evil spirits, then break up the dance and scatter around the Bayou, looking for victims and food. That's the most dreaded time—during the full moon, when unsuspecting strangers or foolish Cajuns wander out into the Bayou.

Older Cajuns often hang flour sifters outside their back doors. They say the loup-garou is compelled to stop and count every hole in the sifter screen. When the creature becomes mesmerized by the sifter, it can be caught. Cajuns then sprinkle salt on the loup-garou, and the salt sets the creature on fire. It sheds its werewolf skin and runs deep into the Bayou, never to return to haunt Cajuns.

Loups-garous are also supposed to be able to change themselves into mules and work their own land during the day, growing black-magic herbs and plants. They are also believed to have huge bats as pets (bats supposedly as big as airplanes!), and these bats carry them anywhere in the Bayou. They even drop loups-garous down chimneys, so they can sneak into bedrooms at night and attack Cajuns while they sleep.

A loup-garou can be killed only one way—with an exorcism. A local priest or traiteur must anoint the ground on which the loup-garou walked. That will remove any evil left behind by the creature, and also prevent it from returning to the house or area. If the loup-garou is caught, it must be anointed with holy water to wash away the evil spirits. The priest reads passages from the Bible, or the traiteur sprinkles the creature with a mixture of herbs and roots (only a Cajun traiteur knows the ingredients of this mixture) and chants. The loup-garou will then resume its human form, whether it was a man or woman, and will slowly die. Cajuns believe this is the only way to kill the creature so it will rest in peace. Bullets, knives, or poisons have no effect. Cajuns also believe that once a loup-garou has been killed, its human name— the name of the person who was transformed into the creature—cannot be spoken for one year from the time of the exorcism, or the speaker will become a loup-garou.

Cajuns ward off the creatures with prayer, holy water, flour sifters, and frogs. Cajuns believe the werewolves are deathly afraid of frogs because of the frog's ties to voodoo as a symbol of bad luck and danger. If you see a loup-garou approaching, you should throw a frog at it; it will run away, never to return. As in all Bayou philosophy, the land creates the illness, and the land provides the cure.

Loups-garous are only the beginning. Cajuns have a legend or superstition for just about anything and everyone—although most of their legends are really an attempt to get children to obey and behave. Cajun children, like most children, are told to put a tooth under their pillow after the tooth falls out. When they're asleep in the middle of the night, a magical creature will come into their room, go under the pillow, take the tooth, and leave money or candy. That magical creature isn't the tooth fairy, but the tooth rat, and it takes the teeth and gives them to other rats in the Bayou. (Maybe the tooth rat is really a nutria?)

Santa Claus comes down from the North Pole every year at Christmas and brings presents to all the good children around the world. In the Bayou, Cajun children celebrate Christmas much the same way other children do, but instead of Santa sliding down the chimney with a bag full of toys, it's Ti-Bonhomme Janvier, Santa Croupee, or Mama

Lee who leaves toys, candy, and goodies on the front porch for the children who have been good throughout the year.

Most American children who are bad are threatened that at Christmas time they will get coal in their stockings or not get the toys they want. Cajun children who misbehave have to pay the price all year. They always have someone watching them, waiting for them to get into trouble. Cajun children who have been especially bad had better be ready for trouble when they go to bed. In the middle of the night, Madame Grandes Doigts (Mrs. Big Fingers) will steal them away and take them to her home deep in the Bayou. There's no escaping from Madame Grandes Doigts; if she catches a bad child, that child will become her slave and live the rest of his life in the deep, dark Bayou, never to see his family or friends again.

If a child isn't really a bad child, but gets into mischief by playing jokes and pranks on people, he'll have to find a way to get away from Con-Jo (conjure man). Con-Jo knows black magic and incantations, and can put certain spells on children, spells that can make them grow warts or turn into frogs—or that can make them be good and never pull pranks again. Con-Jo lurks in the Bayou and comes out at night, peeking in bedroom windows and calling to children from the swamp banks.

Cajun children, like all children, have nightmares from time to time. It's no wonder, with all the mythical creatures roaming the Bayou at night. If a Cajun child has nightmares for several nights in a row, Cajuns say that the child is being haunted by the *letiche,* the soul of an unbaptized baby that died and cannot go to heaven. The soul wanders the Bayou at night, looking for very small children to take over their bodies. Cajuns believe the letiche will never find peace because it has no place to go—there is no place for unbaptized souls after death.

Cajuns say the only way to keep all these bad or evil spirits away during the night is through prayer and belief in God, who is the only thing powerful enough to combat evil while you sleep.

Along with superstitions about evil creatures, there are beliefs dealing with everyday occurrences from drinking coffee to cutting hair. Here are just a few of the Cajun superstitions.

If you drink too much coffee in one day, you will turn darker and darker until you turn black.

If you cut your hair on Good Friday, it will grow back twice as thick.

Be careful of how you dispose of the trimmings from a haircut. If a bird picks them up and uses them for a nest, you will get a strong headache. If a rat finds them good for nesting, you will go crazy.

If you have a wart, prick it with a pin and put the drops of blood from the wart on a grain of corn. Throw the corn to the chickens, and they will get the wart instead of you.

A gold wedding band touched to sore eyes will heal them.

A teething baby may get quick relief if the tooth of a dead Indian is tied around the baby's neck for four days.

The Cajuns are very traditional and have kept centuries-old customs in their modern culture. One of the most popular customs centers around socializing, which is a major aspect of Cajun culture. When the Acadians first settled in Louisiana, they raised livestock for food and trade, much as they did when they lived in Nova Scotia. One of the main animals on Cajun farms in those days was the pig. When it came time to slaughter one of the pigs, the Acadian family found itself with plenty of fresh pork—usually more than the family could eat. Storage was not efficient then, and only dried or smoked pork could be kept for any length of time. So the family invited neighbors over to join the feast. When the other family slaughtered one of its pigs, it would invite another family over, and so on. The event came to be known as a *boucherie* (butchery), and quickly became a Cajun tradition, with many families joining the celebration. Boucheries still go on today, often with whole towns getting in on the festivities. Women prepare breads, sausage (boudin), and rice dishes; men bring beer and coffee.

Holidays are traditional events in southern and southwestern Louisiana, just as they are around the United States and the world. In the Bayou, the Easter season is always kicked off by the Mardi Gras, a time for celebration and fun before the solemn Lenten period begins. On Good Friday before Easter, Cajun families still practice the traditional Catholic day of fasting, with no food or drink for 12 hours before noon. Until that time, Cajuns do not drink coffee or even water; children are not allowed to play or watch television. When Easter finally arrives, the Cajuns attend church dressed in their Easter best. They color eggs, but usually in a more traditional manner than heading to the local store and buying packaged dye. Cajuns boil onion skins and soak the eggs in the water, then etch designs into the shells, ending up with some pretty brown and white Easter eggs. After Mass, Cajun men take part in a quiet game of pock-pocking.

In pock-pocking, two men meet in front of the church. Each one carries brown and white Easter eggs in his pocket. After a friendly greeting, they take the eggs from their pockets and hold them in their hands, usually with the pointed sides out and the round sides buried in the palms of their hands. Then they gently poke one egg into the other, knocking them together until one of the eggs cracks. The cracked egg goes to the man whose egg remained intact. This duel is all in fun, and a Cajun with strong eggs usually ends up with enough winnings to make a pretty good egg salad.

Cajun children don't celebrate Halloween as children do in other parts of the country. Traditionally, they don't wear scary or funny costumes and go door to door for candy. Instead, on the second of November they celebrate All Souls' Day, which is more of a family holiday than something primarily for the children. On All Souls' Day, the families go to the cemetery and pray over the graves of their deceased loved ones. After the prayers, they place flowers at the tombstone and paint the stone white, as a symbol of purity and protection from evil spirits. (When you drive through the Bayou, you'll often see tombstones painted white, a much brighter white than the stone's natural color.) The entire family spends the day remembering the dead and offering prayer so their souls will be at peace.

Children of the Bayou aren't denied the fun and excitement of door-to-door trick-or-treating. Instead of dressing up and going out at the end of October, they wait until New Year's Day. They dress in pleasant costumes, such as princesses or pioneers, not as monsters or space creatures, and their costumes are homemade. They go out not only to collect candy, but also to stop by friends' and neighbors' homes and wish them good luck and prosperity in the new year. They wish them "bonne année," and in turn get homemade breads or crafts or candy.

An old game is still played during the late summer in some of the more rural areas of the Bayou. The game is called the chariot, and it began in the 1800s after a Cajun boy saw a horse-drawn hearse in a funeral procession in New Orleans. The hearse was long and black, with dark curtains. The inside of the hearse was dimly lit with candles, and the light gave off an eerie glow. When the boy got home, he took an old box and poked holes in the sides. He put candles inside the box, knotted a string through the front, and dragged it around the yard. He called it a chariot, and soon his friends began making their own chariot toys, each one getting just a little fancier than the next, with cutouts of stars, moons, hearts, and even names, all glowing in the candlelight.

At first, there was no special time when Cajun children made their chariot toys; they often made them in late summer when darkness began to fall earlier in the Bayou and they were tired of the traditional children's games of jumping rope, marbles, or jacks. Over the years, late summer grew to be the traditional time for the children to make their cutout chariots. Each year the toys were more and more elaborate. The boxes grew from plain, square boxes painted black to fancy churches, castles, or plantationlike cutout boxes. And each year, more and more children participated in the "parade," dragging their chariots down the Bayou roads.

The parade is now a Cajun tradition, with entire families working on each chariot. Many towns, such as St. Martinville, even hold annual chariot parades and award prizes as a major event. Most are held in mid- to late September, and scores of children take part. The theme of each family's chariot is kept secret until the parade. Then the children unveil their chariot and drag it down the street in a long procession through town. The parades are held at dusk, so there is enough light to see the children, yet dark enough for the chariots to give off their eerie candlelight glow.

Perhaps no Cajun customs are more sentimental than those dealing with courtship and marriage. Most Cajun courting customs are still practiced today. Cajuns marry young and have large families, and the families are always close-knit. An unmarried Cajun woman is considered an old maid if she reaches 21 years old with no promise of marriage in the near future. Because Cajuns marry so young, and have an average of six children, it's not unusual to find four and five generations of the same family living in the same town. In fact, one elderly Cajun, a great-great-grandmother, counted 800 members in her family.

Dating in the Bayou is called courting, and when a young man courts a young woman, it's always under the watchful eyes of the woman's parents. When a Cajun boy shows an interest in a girl, he first has to ask permission to court. If permission is granted (and that often depends on the boy's bloodlines and his family's relationship with the girl's family), the boy is invited over to the girl's home for supper. As the men talk, the young woman helps prepare the meal and sets the table, usually within sight of the suitor.

Until recently, the young people would gather on Sunday afternoons after church, or on Saturday, for outdoor parties called *danses rondes*. The purpose was to get young people together, although anyone of any age could attend. The parties would continue all through the day and well into the night.

Traditionally, Cajuns court for a year or two before talking about marriage. When the subject finally arises, and the boy asks the girl for her hand in marriage, it used to be necessary for him to meet the approval of the girl's parents and her grandparents. An older custom, not used as often as it was, uses a third party to speak for the suitor. That third party, usually a friend of the prospective groom, would go to the girl's house and do the talking for the suitor, then return to the suitor with the answer.

When the wedding is announced, usually a month or two before the date, the young woman begins to prepare her trousseau. Older family members would make quilts, knit rugs and blankets, and sew clothes. Friends would bring gifts of mules and chickens. The men would help the future couple prepare their home, either by building a new house or by fixing up an older one in the town.

When the big day finally arrived, the church would be decorated with brightly colored paper flowers. Paper flowers, not real ones, are an old Cajun tradition for several reasons. One is that a florist is too expensive and a waste of money. Another is that the paper flowers can be kept forever and will always be a reminder of the wedding and celebration. The paper flowers are bright and beautiful and never wilt. They are homemade and considered a great gift of someone's time and consideration, showing that someone (usually the godmother) cared enough to spend days on the gift.

The bride always wore a white gown and a long train in a Cajun wedding. The groom always wore a black suit and black gloves. Family and friends invited to the wedding wore their "Sunday" clothes, but never dressed lavishly, keeping all attention focused on the young couple.

After a traditional Catholic ceremony, the newlyweds would hop in a buggy and race back home, followed by their fathers, then the rest of the guests. Sometimes the men would fire their shotguns in the air (similar to honking car horns after the wedding today), and everyone would get ready to eat a hearty supper and dance to Cajun music well into the night. The party was called the *bal de noce*, and its success was judged by how much money the couple received (usually pinned onto their clothes) or by how many cakes and pies were brought to the party by friends.

Weddings are a time of celebration for Cajuns. In the old days, weddings were also a time when the dead were remembered. The Cajun couple would spend their first night together at the home of a neighbor or relative. The next morning, they would go to their new home and begin to unpack their wedding gifts. When things settled down a bit, and the new home was in order, the couple would go to the cemetery. They would kneel beside the grave of the closest relative of the bride and say a prayer. The bride would place her bouquet at the tombstone, so the dead would also be able to share the couple's joy and take part in the festivities. The couple would then go to the grave of the groom's nearest realtive, pray and leave a paper flower at the church. It was believed that with the blessings of the living who actually helped in the celebration, and with the blessings of the dead who received flowers from the ceremony, the newlywed Cajun couple would live a long life together, have plenty of healthy children, and become prosperous.

SAUTER LE BALAI
Il y avait une vieille veuve de Calais,
Qui avait tenté à faire des merveilles.
Avec tous les gris-gris,
Et des poignées du riz,
Pour se faire sauter encore le balai!

JUMP THE BROOMSTICK
There was an old lady from Calais,
Who was trying to do magic.
With all the gris-gris (spells),
And some handfuls of rice,
To jump the broom again!

The broomstick wedding ceremony was once common in the deep Bayou, when no priest was available to marry a young couple. The ceremony was considered a common-law service, and it was perfectly legal and binding. In front of several witnesses from each side, the bride's closest friend and the groom's closest friend would grab hold of opposite sides of a broomstick and hold it about six inches off the floor. The couple would recite the above poem in French, then hop over the broomstick, hand in hand. Everyone would eat and drink and have a good Cajun party. The jump-the-broomstick ceremony is rarely used today, since most areas of the Bayou are more urbanized, and a church and a priest are usually within easy access.

Along with the traditions of Cajun weddings, there are Cajun superstitions on weddings and courtship, most predicting trouble and gloom for the young couple. Here are some of the more common superstitions that have been handed down through the generations.

To determine who will be boss of the house, the older people make a quilt for the girl's trousseau. The young suitor stands on one side of the completed quilt, the young woman on the other. Place a cat on the quilt, and flip it into the air. Whichever side the cat jumps toward determines who will be boss of the new family.

If you dream of death, you will attend a wedding. If you dream of a wedding, you will attend a funeral.

An umbrella placed on a bed will always drive a suitor away from the girl.

If you let a broom sweep your feet, you will not be married for at least another year.

If you sweep your home in the direction of the road, you will sweep away the suitor's love.

If you sweep your home shortly after a suitor visited, you will sweep his love away with him.

It is bad luck to get married unless there is a full moon at the time of the ceremony.

It is bad luck to wear the wedding dress of someone who had been married less than one year. It means the marriage will most certainly end in sorrow.

If you look into a well at noon and see a profile, it is the profile of the person you will marry.

If you look into a well and see a coffin with lighted candles, you will die before your wedding day.

When sewing a wedding gown, be careful of your thread. A knotted thread means there will be trouble in the marriage. A broken thread means the marriage will end in sorrow.

Never give a suitor a knife or a necktie as a gift. A knife means the love affair will be cut off. The necktie means the love will suffocate and die.

A petticoat showing beneath a young girl's skirt means she is available and looking for a husband.

Today, Cajuns are more conventional in their wedding and courting customs. They are still very proper when dating and still hold in respect the family's wishes and permission to get married. But the services look like they could be held anywhere in the United States.

Where Cajun weddings really shine is in the reception. The main purpose is for all the guests to let their hair down and have a lot of fun. There's no pretense about outdoing someone else's wedding or getting the most expensive halls or bands. Cajuns usually have their receptions in the local dance hall, where everyone else in town had theirs. The women in the town usually get together and make the reception dinner in their own kitchens, coming out with some of the best home-cooked food in the Bayou. A whole wall is lined with hot steamtables, loaded with Cajun cakes and pies, rice dishes, shrimp, crawfish, crab, roast pork, and hot boudin. There's always plenty of food, and no one walks away hungry. The Cajun men take care of the drinks and keep the glasses full.

The best part about a Cajun wedding is the music. There's usually an old-fashioned Cajun band playing everything from waltzes to jitterbugs, and everyone dances, young and old. The highlight is the money dance, where the newlyweds waltz together, and as they dance, guests pin money on the clothes of the bride and groom. The money dance usually lasts several minutes, so there's plenty of time for everyone to get involved. By the end of the dance, the bride and groom are literally covered with bills, and everyone's had a chance to introduce themselves or congratulate the new couple. Then it's back to dancing and kicking up the dust until dawn, even though the newlyweds left the reception hours ago.

When the couple first arrived at their new home in the old days, they would "treat" the house for good luck and prosperity. The new bride or her mother went from room to room sprinkling salt. Then she swept out the rooms, beginning in the corner farthest from the door, and working her way toward the door. As she swept, she recited the Lord's Prayer, never saying "Amen" until she had swept the entire house, sweeping the salt out the front door. She then took some fresh salt and lightly sprinkled some on the threshold and under the windowsills. The salt was considered protection, to keep evil spirits out of the house.

When the couple moved in, friends stopped by for a visit, but they never came empty-handed on their first arrival. The usually brought bread (as a symbol of always having something to eat) and wine (so the couple would be fruitful and bear many children).

Although many of these traditional customs are now primarily practiced by the older Cajuns and those still living in the more remote areas of the Bayou, some traditions are still major events in Louisiana. For example, each August, at the opening of the official shrimp season, the Archbishop of New Orleans heads down to the Bayou and blesses the shrimp fleets, both private and commercial. His blessing is considered a symbol of luck and prosperity. Another Cajun custom is never calling another Cajun *monsieur* or *mister*. You use the person's first name, nickname, or no name at all.

In the past two generations, the Acadian people have left centuries-old traditions and customs behind as they tried to move ahead and keep step with the rest of America. Probably the greatest influence on the Cajun people was television, through which they were able to see their differences from the rest of the country. Suddenly, the Cajuns felt backward and illiterate, and many became ashamed of their differences. They began to lose their Cajun-French language, speaking only English. And they began to lose their traditions, customs, and superstitions. As the old fought to keep the old ways, the young fought even harder to change them.

Now the tide seems to be turning back toward the old customs and traditions. As the rest of America searches for its roots, and different cultures try to reestablish their individual uniqueness, many Cajuns are going back to some of the old ways. They are making furniture by hand and braiding their own throw rugs. The children are fascinated by stories of werewolves in the Bayou. Young couples are reincorporating some of the traditional Cajun customs into their marriage ceremonies.

The Cajuns now realize how special a people they really are, and are appreciating their uniqueness. As more and more visitors spend their vacations in southern and southwestern Louisiana, the Cajuns have been getting a greater and greater opportunity to see themselves through the eyes of those who live in crowded, polluted cities where people are rude and life is fast. Now, the Cajuns are looked upon with envy. Their life-style of hard work, hard play, and harmony with nature is certainly a major part of that envy. And so are the simple, graceful Cajun customs and traditions that show men as gentlemen, women as ladies, and the Bayou as a magical, mystical area filled with strange, scary, wonderful creatures.

Folk Tales

Nothing captures the flavor of the Bayou and its people better than age-old folk tales and stories—stories that have been passed down through the generations and cherished as they were told. The Cajun stories explain nature and the seasons (as in mythology), have morals (as do Aesop's fables), or tell about the "old days" of fun and tricks or hardships.

As with most Cajun customs, such as music and cooking, the folk tales and stories are handed down from grandparent to grandchild. Few of the tales have been written down; they are usually remembered and passed on to more people.

Here are some Cajun jokes, stories, folk tales, and old-fashioned tall tales, translated from the "Cajun Radio Storytellers" radio program, broadcast in Cajun-French in the Louisiana area.

STORIES FROM MY GRANDFATHER

as told by David Lanclos of Arnaudville

THE NORTH WIND

Once upon a time, there was a goose and a duck. They were walking together along a very big wall. They walked and walked.

After a while, the goose stopped and turned to the duck. He asked Mister Duck what was behind the big wall. Well, the duck told the goose it was where Mister North Wind lived. The goose said he wanted to meet Mister North Wind. The duck told him, "Oh no. You'd better not disturb him. He's probably sleeping now, and he has a very bad temper. Leave him alone." Well, the goose decided he still wanted to meet the North Wind. So he started with his beak to make a big hole in the wall. He pecked and pecked; all the while the duck kept telling him to stop and not to wake up the North Wind. The goose was very stubborn and kept pecking and finally made a hole in the wall. He started calling, "Mister Wind! Mister North Wind! Wake up! I want to talk to you!" Then he started to yell louder. "Mister Wind! Mister Wind! Wake up! I want to talk with you!" And he did it again and again until the North Wind finally woke up. He was very mad, so he began blowing through the wall. He blew and he blew and he blew. The wind was so strong and so cold that it froze the duck and the goose.

Now every year at this time, the North Wind blows. (This is the same time of year the goose pecked a hole in the wall.) It blows in this country every year now, making everybody cold and miserable. And now when someone is really stupid, the Cajun people say that he is as "stupid as a goose."

THE PROUD GIRL

Once upon a time, there was a very proud Cajun girl. She was so vain and proud and foolish. She also had very bad eyesight . . . blind as a bat, as the saying goes. Well, this girl was so proud that she refused to wear her glasses. She couldn't see a thing without them, but that didn't matter. She didn't want her fiancé to know she had bad eyes because she thought he would think less of her.

One day her fiancé was coming over to her house for a visit. She saw him from a window, when she peeked behind the curtain, and she quickly put her glasses in her pocket so he wouldn't see them. She spent some time with him, and he finally asked her if she would like to go to the *bal* (dance) with him the next night.

She told him, "Yes. It would be very nice." Then her fiancé left, promising to pick her up for the bal the next night.

The next night, she was getting ready, and her father saw her hiding her glasses. Her father thought she was very foolish for being so proud and decided to teach her a lesson. He said, "I see you are going to the bal and you want to impress your fiancé. Here is what I'm going to do to help you. When you are at the bal, I'm going to put a needle in the bush by the house, hidden way away. Then when you are coming toward the front door, you tell your fiancé, 'Oh, look. There is a needle there.' He won't be able to see it, and you are really going to impress him."

So they went to the bal and everything went well, they had a good time. When they were coming back, the proud girl said, "Oh, look. There is a needle there!" The fiancé said, "I don't see anything." But the girl said, "Look. Look right here!" And as she was pointing, she took a step forward, she fell over a cow that was lying there by the front steps. She was so embarrassed that she almost died from shame. And she never saw her fiancé again. (Pride goeth before the fall??)

THE DIVORCE

There was an old man and a foolish old woman who lived together in the Bayou. The woman heard something about some couples getting a divorce. Well, this was something new to the foolish old woman, and she told her husband they should go talk to their parish priest about getting one of those divorces. The woman, of course, had no idea what a divorce was.

When they got to the church, the old woman told the priest to get them a divorce. The priest was shocked, because in the Catholic religion (especially in those days) you never got a divorce. The only way to separate from your spouse was by death. The priest decided that if the old man and the foolish old woman really wanted a divorce, he would give them one. So he opened his Bible and read and read and read. Then he closed the book and hit the old woman on the head. The old woman was shocked, but didn't say anything because she thought this was part of the divorce.

Then the priest turned to the old man and hit him on the head. He just looked at his wife. Then the priest hit the old woman on the head again. Then he hit her again. Finally the foolish old woman jumped up and asked the priest why he was hitting her in the head. The priest said that it was the only way he could give them a divorce, because the only way was by death. Well, the old woman was shocked. She said, "If that's the only way I can get a divorce, then I don't want one! We changed our mind!"

A SNAKE GOES FISHING

Once upon a time, there was a young Cajun man who went fishing in the Bayou. He was out in the Bayou all day and didn't catch anything. He didn't want to go home empty-handed, and he didn't know what to do. When he was about to leave, he saw a large snake with a big frog in its mouth. The fisherman called for the snake to come over by his boat. The stupid snake swam over to the boat, carrying the frog in its mouth. (The frog was the snake's dinner, you see.) The fisherman asked the snake if he could have his frog so he wouldn't go home empty-handed. The snake gave the fisherman his frog. The fisherman was so grateful that he wanted to repay the snake for its kindness. All the fisherman had was a bottle of wine, so he pulled out the cork from the bottle and opened the snake's mouth. He poured the wine down the snake's throat, and the snake swam off.

Then the fish started coming around and the fishing got to be very good. The fisherman caught all sorts of fish, more than he could ever want. As he was about to leave, he saw the snake swim up to his boat again. The snake was carrying another frog in its mouth. You see, the snake wanted to trade his dinner for another drink of wine, and was willing to go hungry just for a drink. But the fisherman didn't need another frog, so the snake stayed thirsty.

JACKRABBIT AND THE ALLIGATOR

There was a jackrabbit who liked to go looking for food. He liked to eat vegetables and things, and he knew there was a big vegetable garden on the other side of the Bayou. But the water in the Bayou was too deep, and the jackrabbit knew he could not get across the water. The jackrabbit looked around trying to figure out what to do. He saw some alligators in the water, lying around in the sun, being lazy. The jackrabbit looked at the alligators and found an old one that could barely see. The rabbit went up to the old alligator and said, "Good morning, Mister Alligator." And Mister Alligator replied, "Good morning, Mister Rabbit."

The rabbit moved closer to the alligator and said, "You know, I would really like to count you, but you and your friends are so spread apart that I always lose count. I have an idea. Why don't you get all the alligators together and lie one next to the other, all across the Bayou. Then I can step over you one at a time, and it will be very easy to count you."

The alligators did just that—lined up side by side across the Bayou—and the jackrabbit hopped across, acting as if he were counting each alligator. Fairly quickly, he was reaching the other side of the Bayou. When he got to the last alligator, he stopped and turned to him and said, "You foolish alligator. I didn't want to count you. I just wanted to get across the Bayou and used you to help me get across!"

The last alligator became so enraged that he opened his big jaws and took a big bite from the rabbit's tail. (You see, before this, rabbits used to have very long tails.) When the alligator closed his jaws, he bit very hard, biting the rabbit's tail off, leaving him only with a very fluffy ball. And that is why jackrabbits now have short tails!

CRACK THE FLEA

Once upon a time, there was an old man and a stupid old woman. The woman loved to *craker la puce* (crack or kill the flea, meaning to argue). She would argue and argue with her husband over anything and at any time. If her husband said something was black, she would say it was white, just to be able to argue with the old man. They would go outside and she would argue, always picking fights over anything. The man was getting more and more mad at the old lady.

One day, the old lady started to pick another fight with the old man, and argued and argued about nothing. The man got so mad that he picked up the old woman and threw her into the well. The old woman went down the well, and the water slowly started rising. He asked the old woman, "Are you going to stop?" The old woman said, "No, I love to craker la puce. I have so much fun craker la puce that I will go on forever." And while she said this, she scraped her forefinger against her thumbnail (as if to kill the flea). The old man looked over the edge of the well, and would ask the old woman every so often, "Are you going to stop? Are you going to stop?" The woman kept answering, "No! I will always craker la puce!" And she made the gesture again with her fingers.

Well, the water kept rising, and she was beginning to drown. Her husband said, "You are drowning, you stupid old woman. Now will you stop arguing and save your life?" The old woman still told him, "No. This is what I like." The water now rose over her head, and she drowned. But as she went under the water, her two hands rose up above the surface. The old man saw this and said, "Now you will drown because you won't stop arguing." At that, the old woman's two hands scratched the forefingers against the thumbnails as if to craker la puce for the last time. You see, the old woman got in the very last word before she died.

THE STINKING BEAST

Two companions (animals) were walking through the Bayou one day, and they were arguing between themselves. They were wondering which one of them was the stronger of the two. They both thought that they were stronger than the other. But they didn't really want to get into a fight to find out because they were both so strong that they would really get hurt and destroy each other. So they thought and thought and thought of how they could find out who was the strongest of the two. They decided the best way to find out was to go and ask Mister Owl, because Mister Owl was very wise and very knowledgeable. So the two companions walked through the Bayou until they found Mister Owl.

When they found Mister Owl, they asked him who was the strongest. Mister Owl thought and thought and said, "Well, I cannot decide that by myself. So I will go over and ask the other animals here and see if they might know the answer."

One animal said, "One is stronger because he has black fur and black eyes and he looks very strong." Another one said, "Yes, he is big, but the other one is so tall and so solid that he must be the stronger of the two." Mister Owl was not getting anywhere, and he walked back to the two companions and told them they had to fight to solve their problem.

The two companions began to fight, agreeing that if it was a decision of Mister Owl, that is what they would do. They fought. While they were fighting, there was a little skunk in the earth. The little guy started coming out and he was really mad because they woke him up. He said, "Hey, who's disturbing my sleep?" and he saw those two big ones fighting. He was very mad now, and he let it be known that he was very mad, and the little animal started running and running and running all around the place of the two fighters. The two companions stopped fighting.

The moral of the story is that it's not always the one who looks the strongest, or the tallest, or the biggest who is the most powerful. The stinking beast was certainly the one who was the most powerful of the animals, though he was the smallest.

THE SUN HEATER

There's an old Cajun story about why we have so many good warm days here in the Bayou. An old grandfather was on the front porch talking to his little grandson. He said, "Probably today Theophite is the sun heater." (Theophite was a person's name.) The grandson looked puzzled at the grandfather because he did not understand. The grandfather said that in the old days when there were very, very good men who were working and they would die, we used to say, "Well, God will choose him as a sun heater," because he was so good on earth. The day was so hot that the grandfather was sure that the day was the one set aside by God for his friend to be the sun heater. (The warm days are considered to be very good, and they are a gift of the soul from a good person who died to those who remained on earth.)

A STRONG STORY

There were three farmers, Gaston, Louis, and Pierre. The first one said, "I used to raise chickens. The chickens were raised right next to my other field. And that was a field of hot peppers. The chickens used to eat my peppers. One day, when my wife went to kill a chicken for dinner, it was so strong, we could not eat the chickens."

Well, Louis heard the story and said, "Well, that's nothing compared to my story! I was also raising chickens in a field right next to hot peppers, and my chickens would also eat those peppers all the time. When they started to lay eggs, the eggs hatched right away, instead of taking 21 days, because the peppers were so hot. The eggs just popped right open and I had new chickens!"

Pierre listened to both stories, and he joined in. Pierre said, "Well! That's *nothing* like my chickens. You should have seen *my* chickens. I also raised my chickens next to my hot pepper field. They also ate so many hot peppers. They ate and ate and ate. Then one night, I saw a fire coming from the chicken coop. It was a big fire with smoke and everything. Those crazy chickens had become so hot, they burned down the whole henhouse!"

THE DISHMOP SOUP

There was an old man who loved to eat. His passion was eating, and he would eat all day and all night. Just eat and eat, even in the middle of the night. One night he woke up, and he was very hungry. He saw a large pot near the stove and opened the cover and looked inside. He said to himself, "Oh, good. The old woman has made some soup for me to eat." The old man got out a ladle and spooned out two big spoonfuls. But the soup was terrible, and he found that he was not able to eat a big, hard thing that was in the soup.

The old man was angry. He walked back into the bedroom and woke his wife up from her sleep. He said, "Old woman, why does your soup taste like soap, and why can't I eat this thing? It's so hard!" "You fool," said the old wife, "this was my dishmop which I put in hot soap to soak at night. This will teach you not to eat at night!" The old man never woke up to eat again.

THE ACADIAN GIRL

There was this Acadian girl who lived at home with her very, very old grandfather. He was ready to die, so one day he called his granddaughter over to his bed. He said, "You know, I am going to die." The little girl was very sad and said, "No, grandfather. I don't want you to die." He said, "Yes, I must. I am very old and I am going to die." But he had one request before he died. He said, "I would like to smoke my pipe for the last time." The granddaughter handed him his pipe, and she looked around for something to light the pipe with. She couldn't find matches because they were so poor and had none in the house.

The fire in the fireplace was almost out, but there were still some hot embers in the bottom. While the little Acadian girl was looking for something to light her grandfather's pipe, she saw the embers, and thought they would be useful to light the pipe. But now she could not find anything to take the hot embers from the fireplace with, so she would not burn herself. So what she did was put a little bit of ashes in her hand, making a little cup in her hand. Then she put a hot ember in the ashes, and the ashes stopped the ember from burning her hand. She brought them to her grandfather. Her grandfather looked at the little girl and was amazed. He said, "Well, I am ready to die, I am an old man, but I was still able to learn something new." (He learned how to hold hot embers in his hand.)

PRACTICAL JOKERS AT THE DANCE
as told by Felix Richard of Cankton

In the old days, bals (dances) were rough, and trouble often broke out—fights and shouting. And there were a lot of practical jokes being played.

In the old days, a father didn't encourage his son to go to the bals to dance. A father told his son, "You are too young to go to the bal and jump with the girls. [The Cajun term for dancing translates literally to "jump with the girls."] If you go, you will meet a girl and fall in love. You have to be prepared because it will lead to marriage and you have nothing to your name. And how could you support a wife? You don't even own a buggy!" So this son stayed with his father year after year. The father gave the son a portion of his cotton and cornfields. The young son worked these fields and eventually began putting some money on the side. He got more and more money as the years went on, and each year he would ask his father if he could yet go to the bal. But the father still thought his son was not yet prepared because he still had nothing to his name.

The son decided one day that he finally had enough money to buy a horse and a buggy, which were considered a big status symbol. But he didn't just buy any horse and buggy. He bought the best horse and the best buggy he could find. Finally, his father told him that he had such a fine *équipage* (horse and buggy) that he should go to the bal. The father said, "Yes, Alphonse. You are ready now to go and jump with the girls. However, let me give you some warning. Remember, when you go to the bal, a lot of practical jokes are played. Go only if you will be careful where you leave your horse and buggy, and check on your horse and buggy from time to time."

The son left. When he got to the hotel where the bal was going to take place, he parked his horse and buggy by a light pole because it was night. And when he went inside he danced and danced, from time to time checking on his équipage. The son was good-looking and very much in demand.

It was hot at the bal, and he was sweating. Each time he went out to check on his équipage, he took a sip of liquor from a jar. And one time when he went to check on his équipage, he became quite shocked at the sight in front of him. Someone had painted his horse green! He rushed back to the bal and ran up to the playing band and made the players stop, demanding silence and asking who had done such a thing to his beautiful horse.

A big, heavy man, a *boulet* (bully), approached the orchestra slowly. He wore black pants and a white shirt, with the buttons unbuttoned all the way to his belly button. Planting himself by the band, he said, "I did it. Do you have any complaints?" Alphonse remained silent for a while, reflecting. He didn't have any idea that the giant, the boulet, had done it. After reflecting, he said to the boulet, "Well, the first coat is dry. It is now ready for the second coat!" (The bully didn't know what to say and did not get the fight he hoped for.)

I used to sleep at my grandma's when I was 15 or 16 or so. She lived alone; she was in her 80s. What a memory she had. She used to tell me this story. . . .

Both neighbors on each side had large families, and both had a son of the same age. Each young man had a horse and a buggy, as was the custom in those days, and they would both attend the evening bal. Well, those two *greddins* (joke-players) both loved the same girl—a pretty little thing who loved them both and could not decide between the two. So the two men used to take turns dancing with her at the bal. And it was like that for quite a while.

But one day at the bal, one of the young men became very jealous. So he left the bal and went outside where the horses and buggies were parked and decided to play a bad joke on his friend. He cut off the tail of his friend's fine horse. Then he went back to the bal and began to dance with the girl. The second lad went outside and noticed what had happened to his horse. He knew it was his friend who had played this bad joke on him. He said, "Well, I'm going to pay him back," and took his knife and made a good joke. He went back to the bal, and when it was his turn, he started to dance with the girl.

But the girl began to notice the jealousy between the two lads, and she decided she had had enough and wanted to leave. So they left. While the two lads were walking with their horses on their way home, the first young man said to the second, "By the way, did you notice someone played a bad joke on your fine horse and cut his tail?" The second lad didn't say anything for a while, but then replied, "Oh, of course. But did you notice on your own horse what happened? He has been laughing ever since we left!"

You see, the second lad had cut the other horse's lips, so all its teeth were showing, and that's why the horse was laughing at the good joke.

TALL TALES OF HUNTING
as told by Felix Richard of Crankton

THE BEST HUNT EVER

In the old days, hunters didn't hunt for the fun of it; they hunted because they needed meat. There was an old Cajun man and his wife. The Cajun man was a hunter. One day his wife said to him, "You have to go and hunt in the Bayou because we need meat to eat." So the old man took his hunting rifle and his hunting knife with him and went out into the Bayou to hunt for some meat.

He wandered deep in the Bayou, looking for some game to hunt for food. After a while, he saw a deer way off in the distance. He thought, "Aha!" and thought he would shoot the deer for meat. But then he noticed an alligator in the water of the Bayou. He thought that it, too, would make a good dinner. So he thought, "What to do? I have two animals that I can eat for dinner. I would like to have them both. But if I kill the deer with my gun, the alligator will swim away because he would be frightened by the shot. If I shoot the alligator, the deer will surely run away where I will never catch him. What will I do?"

So the old man sat down and thought and thought and thought of how he could get both animals at one time. After thinking awhile, he came up with a way. He took out his hunting knife and took out a bullet from the gun. He tossed the bullet up into the air, and split the bullet in half with his knife. When he fired the bullet from the gun, it went off in both directions—one at the deer, the other at the alligator. Each was hit by the half-bullet and fell. So his idea worked. Almost. The old hunter saw that the deer was not completely killed.

The deer was badly wounded and went off into the water of the Bayou to try to swim away. The hunter wanted to follow the deer and finish it so he could bring it back home along with his alligator. So as the deer swam through the Bayou, the hunter followed it into the water.

The hunter took off his shoes and held them at his sides, under the water, as he swam in the Bayou. As he caught up with the deer at the other end of the Bayou, the hunter found out the deer had died. As the hunter stood up to get the deer, he bent down to put on his shoes, and what do you know? Not only did the old hunter have the deer and the alligator, but his shoes were all filled with fish! What a fisherman he was and what a hunter he was! Well, the old hunter was so happy that he lifted his hands in the air, high above his head, to thank God for his good fortune. And as he was doing so, there were two wild geese passing by. And what do you know? The old hunter went home with the deer, the alligator, two geese, and a whole lot of fish. And he was certainly the best hunter in all the Bayou and went on his best hunt ever.

THE QUAIL-HUNTING MULE

Mister Louis lived in the Bayou, and he was a very good hunter. He went hunting quite often. Well, Mister Louis had a very strange animal on his farm, a mule that thought it was a hunting dog! You should have seen this "dog." If Mister Louis would take his fishing gear and go out to fish, the "dog" would do nothing. But if Mister Louis would take his gun to go hunting, how the "dog" would get excited. It would do all sorts of things, wanting to go on the hunt. This mule, you see, was a very good hunting "dog."

In the village, there was this pharmicist and this doctor, and they wanted to go hunting. They were very inexperienced at hunting and did not know where to go for the best hunting. They wanted to hunt quail. So they asked Mister Louis where he thought the best places were to go hunt quail. Mister Louis knew the two men knew nothing about hunting, but he told them anyway, "Look, you bring your two dogs and go to this place in the Bayou. If you go there you are sure to have a good hunt."

The two men went out into the Bayou and looked and looked and looked for quail. They spent the whole day looking but came back empty-handed. They could not catch anything. They were very angry, and they went back to the village to find Mister Louis. When they found him, they told him all about their hunting trip, and how the place he told them to go was no good because they didn't shoot any quail. Well, Mister Louis had enough of these two men and decided to "help" them out. He said, "Well, I tell you what. I will help you. Come back tomorrow, but don't bring your dogs. You see over there in my yard? You see my mule?" The two men looked and saw the mule and said, "Yes, we see your mule." They were confused. Mister Louis explained, "You see, that mule is the very best hunting dog in the Bayou." The two men looked at each other and couldn't believe it. But they thought they'd go along with the story.

The next morning, the two men arrived at Mister Louis's home, and he introduced them to the mule, and told the mule to go help the men hunt for quail. As the two men walked through the Bayou with the mule, quail would fly everywhere! Every time the mule would take a step, a flock of quail would jump up into sight. (You see, the quail stay near the ground and the two hunters were first looking for them in the sky. They didn't know the mule was walking through the quail nests, disturbing the quail.) Well, the two hunters were getting quail everywhere, and soon their bags were just filled with the birds.

When they could hold no more, the two hunters stopped for a while and started talking. They thought that since they were such good hunters, maybe they would be good fishermen, too. So they proudly returned the "dog" to Mister Louis, and boasted of their catch with the fine hunting "dog." Well, Mister Louis thought this was all very funny because the two men didn't know that a trick was played on them. When the two men started telling how they would like to be great fishermen, Mister Louis again played a joke. He told the men, "Well, if you think my dog is such a good hunter, wait until you take him along and see him fish!"

THE CAPERS WE PULLED
as told by Coon Picou and Loulan Pitre of Cut Off

Mister Picou lived in Grand Isle, and tells about how he worked on the boats loading and unloading cotton and rice along the Mississippi River, and some of the pranks that were pulled in those early days.

THE HORSEMEAT AND THE FLIES

One day two men were coming back from working along the river, and they were walking down the road. As they were walking, they saw a small type of restaurant, and decided to stop in and see what it was all about. Inside was this stranger who wasn't a Cajun because he didn't speak any Cajun or French. But this man was holding a very big platter. On the platter were steak and potatoes, and it looked very good. So the two workers thought for a minute, and decided to stay at the restaurant. The stranger invited the men inside to stay and told them, "Please stay. Eat. Look, I made some very good steak for you!"

Well, the two men started to eat. But after a few moments, Coon Picou became very suspicious and didn't want to eat any more, and he ended up only tasting a little bit. You see, he thought there was something wrong because the stranger was so eager to get them to eat his steak. When the meal was finished, the stranger, whose name was George, started laughing. He told them, "You know what you have been eating? You have been eating horsemeat!" George laughed, but the two men were angry at the trick that had been played on them.

A few weeks later, the two men decided to play a joke on George and get back at him for his mischief. They invited George over to eat some hamburger with them. When Coon Picou took his skillet and began to cook the "hamburger," it was really full of flies and worms and not ground meat. Coon Picou cooked the meat, adding a little grease and such, and mixed it all very well so it looked good. When George came over for dinner, Coon Picou served it to him.

George ate the mixture. When the meal was all done, Coon Picou said to George, "Do you know what you ate? You ate worms and flies, not hamburger as we had said it was!" Well, George was so mad that he didn't speak to the two men for two weeks! They got George back for his joke on them.

THE FIDDLE AND THE FIDDLERS

as told by Lionel Leleux of Leleux

Mister Leleux was a fiddle player and tells of life at the bals in the late 1920s, when he was onstage as a performer.

At the bal, the old people and the children stayed on the benches. The men would have to buy a ticket to get into the dance, and they usually paid for their girl to go to the bal (or the women would get in free). When the music started, you would walk in the middle of the floor to meet your girl. When the music stopped, you would let your girl go back and sit down on the other side of the room.

In those days, if you had 35¢ for the dances, you were rich. It cost 25¢ to buy the ticket and 10¢ to buy the drink. If you had a girl and had 10¢, it was wonderful because you could dance and take a drink to your girl. You had to have money to treat your girl in those days. In the old days, you had to leave the floor after the music stopped, and you bought your girl a drink. But today, we are allowed to stay and talk during intermission if we want to, and now we do that mostly. The custom has also changed and now the girl can stay with her boyfriend during the whole dance, and not leave for opposite sides of the room.

If it was discovered that someone in the dance hall had a bottle of booze in his pocket, it was reported to the musicians, and the musicians had to ask the offender to leave. You see, no one was allowed to carry booze on the dance floor.

Life has changed a lot. Now people go to the bal, but there is no trouble like it used to be. A long time ago, there was a man at the bal who had been getting into trouble—he had been making a bad joke on someone. Everyone at the dance got mad at him, and started to bombard him with stones. (The troublemaker was the guitar player in the band.) Well, the troublemaker was getting hit with the stones, and the stones were hitting his guitar and bouncing off. He even started swatting the stones with his guitar! Well, this man was jumping all around the dance floor, trying not to get hit with stones. He finally jumped out of a window to get away from the stones. All the while he was running, he kept playing his

guitar. And you know what song he played? "Home Sweet
Home," all the while he was running fast!

Musicians used to play sitting down sometimes in the old days.
There was this one fiddler who used to take requests from the
people at the bal. He would tell them, "If you can whistle the
tune, I can play it. I can play anything you ask for."

One day, in the middle of the bal, the zipper on the musician
became undone. The men and women at the bal became kind of
embarrassed and didn't know how to tell the man that his zipper
was undone. After much talk among the people, one man went up
to his wife and said, "Why don't you go up and tell him?" Gently,
the wife went up to the musician to tell him about the problem.
Very shyly and very embarrassed, she told the man, "Sir, your zipper is open!" Thinking it was a request for a song, the musician
smiled and replied, "If you can whistle it, I can play it!"

And so the jokes and stories go, handed down from generation to
generation with love and care in the Bayou. Cajuns say that their
stories tend to lose a lot of things in the translation to English—most
important the feeling that the Cajuns put into their stories, the flow of
the language, the expressions that are unique to Acadia, and the way
their voice inflections add to the stories. It is impossible to capture the
flavor of these Cajun stories without being able to hear—and understand—them in the native Cajun.

Cajun is not an easy language to learn. It is considered a bastardiza-
tion of the common French language. Words are run together, mispronounced; expression is changed; old and antiquated words and
expressions are used. The language has never been written. The farmers and peasants who lived in Nova Scotia nearly 250 years ago were
isolated, and the language has changed little since then. Each person
added a few mispronunciations and little grammatical quirks as he
passed the language along to his children. And those children, in turn,
added their own differences and passed them along. But the Cajun
language is still the old French, with some changes.

Today, many Cajuns are pushing to revive the Cajun language. One
of the efforts is through a local radio series, where old Cajun storytellers sit and chat and relate experiences, or share stories that have been

passed down to them. Each program has the same theme—remember the Cajun language and pass it along to your children; keep the heritage strong.

Here is the closing theme of the radio program; it sums up the struggle to keep the Cajun language alive (translated from the Cajun-French).*

Here in south Louisiana
For a very long time now,
We've had evening visits with our friends.

Mom and the kids all around,
Dad told stories.
We had a good time sitting out on the porch.

But for a while we forgot.
They tried to eradicate our French.
The Cajun and the Creole stories were no longer in style.

But here we are hearing them again.
The radio, and us on either side of it,
Listening to Louisiana's storytellers.

*Cajun folk tales courtesy of Cote-Blanche Productions, Cut Off, Louisiana.

THROUGH THE BACK DOOR

Touring Acadiana

W<small>HEN YOU'RE HEADING DOWN</small> to southern and southwestern Louisiana, plan on spending a lot of time because there is a lot to see and do. The state is filled with old nineteenth-century mansions and plantations and Acadian homes, each one housing antiques and artifacts from the period. A walk through any of the old homes or plantations gives you a real feel for the history of the Bayou with a firsthand look at how the early Cajuns lived, worked, and played. The early tools, clothes, and cooking utensils show the hardships of early life in the Bayou, and how the Cajuns made the most of what little they had.

Many of the plantations are pre–Civil War era and still have slave quarters in the rear. In fact, some of the old plantations are still being used, and the slave quarters have been converted into overnight lodging for guests and travelers. Privately owned plantations usually don't have tours or are not open to the public, but some Cajuns will open their doors to strangers if approached in just the right way.

The Bayou is also an area with scores of museums. There's a museum in almost every city, and most of the museums are quite impressive, filled with antiques and historic documents about the individual town or parish, donated by local residents. Most are free, and they're usually the best place to begin a tour of an individual town. They're

153

also a good way to meet local residents and learn about the good "hidden away" spots that make a vacation memorable.

A wide variety of Acadian homes have been restored and furnished. Some are at least 250 years old, and are nothing more than one-room cabins built from Louisiana Bayou-area cypress trees. Moss-stuffed mattresses and furniture have been preserved and are on display in the rooms, along with handmade tables, chairs, and tools. Some homes are mansions, filled with art treasures and museum pieces, all in full view and out in the open without glass or plastic obstructing the view.

If you're looking for a little more adventure in the form of hunting, fishing, or just plain roughing it for a few days, many of the towns bordering the swamps offer guided tours of the marshlands. Some management areas have been carefully preserved and remain untouched by development. You can see wild animals in their natural habitat, and get a closeup look at how the Bayou animals live. Some areas are only accessible by boat, and Cajuns advise you not to go in unless you're with a Cajun guide.

Acadiana is a large, bountiful, and varied area of Louisiana. Covering the southern and southwestern regions of the state, each of the seven Bayou areas is markedly different from the others, with each one establishing its own reputation based on its vegetation, waterways, marshlands, hunting, fishing, or attractions. The seven areas are: Imperial-Calcasieu Territory, Courtableau Country, Teche-Vermilion Country, Les Trois Rivieres, Atchafalaya Basin, Mississippi River Region, and Lafourche-Terrebonne Bayouland.

Imperial-Calcasieu Territory is the most western of the seven Acadian territories, bordered by Texas on the west, Jennings and Lake Arthur on the east, and De Quincy and Elton on the north. The area is mainly known for its fishing and wildfowl, and visitors can also hike through thousands of miles of nature trails and wild animal refuges. Calcasieu Lake is famous for its blue crabs, trout, redfish, and flounder. The town of Cameron is a monument to courage and strength; it was totally rebuilt after a devastating hurricane in 1957 that killed more than 500 residents. It is now one of the country's leading commercial fishing ports. The main highways through Imperial-Calcasieu are Highway 82, which runs along the Gulf, and Highway 27, which cuts vertically through the territory. Its main towns are Sulphur, Lake Charles, and Jennings. Happy hunting!

To the north is Courtableau Country, which is sectioned by Evangeline to the west, Turkey Creek to the north, Lebeau and Arnaudville to the east, and Rayne and Morse to the south. This area is where to find real down-home Cajun music. There's the Happy Landing in Pecaniere in St. Landry Parish, where you might see a Cajun wedding. Fred's Lounge in Mamou is a Cajun music legend, and the Step-Inn Club in Lawtell is one of the oldest of the Cajun music clubs. Major cities in Courtableau Country are Crowley, Rayne, Opelousas, Ville Platte, Eunice, and Mamou. It's the place to go for a lively Saturday night in the Bayou.

If you're looking to try some hot, spicy Cajun cooking, head straight south to Teche-Vermilion Country, where Cajuns believe you'll find some of the best food in the world. This area is bordered by Gueydan and Duson to the west, Carencro and Henderson to the north, Lake Fausse Point to the east, and the Gulf to the south. Right in the heart of Teche-Vermilion Country is the heart of all Acadiana—Lafayette. There you'll find plenty of good restaurants serving mounds of boiled crawfish along with a side order of Cajun music. Try the Cafe Vermilionville or Chez Pastor or Toby's Oak Grove. Jacob's at Four Corners in Lafayette is famous for its Shrimp de la Teche. Major cities in Teche-Vermilion are Lafayette, Broussard, Breaux Bridge, Abbeville, New Iberia, St. Martinville, and Delcambre.

An area ribboned with streams and rivers—and a fisherman's paradise—is the Les Trois Rivieres territory, bordered by Bunkie and Morrow to the west, Lottie and Lakeland to the south, and the Mississippi River to the east. The False River to the east offers some of the best sailing, waterskiing, and bluegill and bass fishing in the state. The scenic drive along the river is a good place to get away on a Sunday afternoon. One of the first posts established in Louisiana was in Pointe Coupee, near the lake. The area is also famous for its vast collection of Civil War–era homes and river's-edge plantations, many of which have been restored and are open to the public. Some of the larger cities in the area are New Roads, St. Francisville, and Simmesport. The most important landmarks in the territory are the three rivers—Atchafalaya, Mississippi, and Red—that cut through Les Trois Rivieres, giving the region its name.

The stouthearted and rugged should find the ultimate challenge due east, in the Atchafalaya Basin, considered one of America's last great remaining swampland wilderness areas. Right in the middle of

Acadiana, the Basin is free and open, with only a few small towns along its marsh banks, and Interstate 10 (called the Swamp Expressway in this area) slicing through the upper portion. In the Basin you'll find miles and miles of untamed Bayou country, filled with thousands of wild birds and waterfowl, fish, and game. Many Cajuns believe the Basin is still the home of rare animals, most believed to be extinct. Deep in the Basin is nature as it was meant to be, following its natural cycle without human interference. Take a Cajun guide if you're looking for some good hunting, fishing, or sightseeing.

The Mississippi River Region is due east. Here is where time kicked off its shoes and settled back against the grace and style of the Old South. Bordered by Plaquemine to the west, Donaldsonville and Des Allemands to the south, New Orleans to the east, and Baton Rouge to the north, the Mississippi River Region is filled with antebellum mansions and moss-covered cypress trees swaying over the river's edge. Hollywood often comes to this region when looking for just the right plantation or mansion for a movie. Ashland-Belle Helene, about six miles past Geismar, was the site for *Band of Angels* with Clark Gable and *The Beguiled* with Clint Eastwood. Houmas House at Darrow welcomed Bette Davis in *Hush Hush, Sweet Charlotte* and James Franciscus in the television series "Longstreet." It was the pattern for Tara in *Gone with the Wind.* Some of the towns along the Mississippi River are Port Allen, St. James, Geismar, Gramercy, Vacherie, and Norco.

No trip to the Bayou is complete without taking a look at the shrimp boats and driving down narrow pontoon bridges and roads nestled right against the Bayou's edge. The place to see miles of winding bayous and meet friendly Cajun people is the Lafourche-Terrebonne Bayouland, the farthest south of the Acadian territories. There, you can take Annie Miller's Swamp Tour and come face to face with Bayou chickens, alligators, and giant snakes. The entire area is fragmented with bayous, some deep and used by commercial shrimpers and oil ships, others dark and shallow where only a small pirogue can work its way through. Perhaps no area in Acadiana is more typical of the stereotyped "Bayou," and it's everything a visitor would expect. Some of the towns in Lafourche-Terrebonne Bayouland are Thibodaux, Houma, Chauvin, Cut Off, Golden Meadow, and Grand Isle.

One of the major resources in the Bayou is oil, and dotted throughout the area are slow-pumping oil wells. Along any of the highways in

Acadiana you can see small rigs steadily pumping in front yards, open fields, and by the road. The oil industry has saved the Cajuns during recent recessions, keeping thousands of families fed. The center of the oil industry is in Lafayette, where more than 800 oil companies and firms have district or regional headquarters. The oil industry has sparked related industries, such as manufacturing, geology, drilling firms, and oil shipping. The Gulf of Mexico is within easy access from almost anywhere in the Bayou, and on any given day, you'll see huge oil tankers docked in port, waiting either to load or unload a shipment.

When driving along the inner roads of Acadiana, you'll also see acres and acres of cotton fields. Cotton is another big industry in southern and southwestern Louisiana, as it is throughout most of the South. Next to rice and sugarcane, cotton is one of the oldest industries in the region; it helped the Acadians earn a prosperous livelihood when they first began settling the Bayou area. A short drive off the major highways will take you to working cotton mills, where you can see the milling process from beginning to end, and where you can buy crafts made from the local Louisiana cotton.

One of the most surprising things you'll see when touring Acadiana, especially if you're there during a local election, is the Cajun method of campaigning. Scattered along telephone poles and store windows are campaign posters, similar to those you'd find in almost any small town in America . . . except for one peculiar difference. Most of the candidates don't specify their party affiliation. The posters feature a picture of the candidate, who usually has a typical Cajun name, and under the picture will be a quote or saying about the candidate's position; you'll really have to look to find the party. In Acadiana, the people say they vote for the person and not the party, and the towns are so small everyone knows the candidates or their families.

Shopping is a pleasure in the small towns of Acadiana. Pull off any main road and head through any town. You'll find wonderful fresh-baked breads and cakes at bakeries chock-full of some of the most unusual foods you'll ever see. Small stores sell handmade Cajun crafts, and antique stores have prices well below big-city prices, many with rare, one-of-a-kind pieces, or antiques from the Old South. Going to small towns is also a good way to meet friendly Cajun people who will probably direct you to some out-of-the-way places. Stop in any shop or restaurant, and get ready to make new friends.

Interstate 10 cuts across the state and is probably the best starting point to locate these small towns and Bayou areas. Here is a list of some towns and what they have to offer. It's only a beginning. When you're there, ask around for places that are off the beaten path. Have fun and welcome to Acadiana!

ABBEVILLE

Steen Syrup Mill. Raw sugarcane is made into syrup from mid-October through the end of December, still using the open-kettle boiling method.

Riviana Rice Mills. One of the largest rice-milling facilities in the United States.

ATCHAFALAYA BASIN

Butte La Rose. The only major settlement within the levees of the floodway. The Basin contains over 800,000 acres of hardwood forests, cypress swamps, marshes, and bayous, and is considered the last great wilderness left in the nation. It is also one of the few places where black bears exist, along with alligators, wildfowl, and game. A guide is strongly advised.

CAMERON

Creole Nature Trail. Hundreds of thousands of acres of untouched wetlands, through southern Calcasieu and Cameron parishes, to the Gulf of Mexico, filled with wildlife and natural Bayou trails.

CENTERVILLE

Marsh Island Refuge. On Marsh Island south of Vermilion Bay are 82,000 acres accessible only by boat in rough terrain. It is a refuge for wild geese, ducks, and other birds, alligators, muskrat, mink, raccoons, and otters. It has no facilities; guides are strongly recommended.

CHAUVIN

La Tourvaille. A quaint, simple Cajun museum with historical artifacts about Bayou Lafourche, complete with gift shop and Cajun meals served on selected days.

CONVENT

St. Michael's Church. Built in 1809, the church houses a replica of the grotto of Lourdes. The exterior dome of the church was made from an inverted sugar kettle.

CROWLEY

Crowley Historic District. Listed in the national register, the district has 382 buildings from the late nineteenth and early twentieth century, considered some of the best period architecture.

Rice Museum. Exhibits on Acadian culture, the rice industry, and town history, with equipment and early Acadian relics and a working rice mill.

Blue Rose Museum. Antebellum Acadian cottage built in 1848 contains old kitchen equipment, tools, china, and antiques.

DONALDSONVILLE

Sunshine Bridge. The only ferry bridge between Baton Rouge and New Orleans, named for the song "You Are My Sunshine."

Lafitte's Landing. Raised cottage built in 1797, believed to have been a resting place for pirate Jean Lafitte.

ELTON

Coushatta Indian Trading Post. Cultural center contains a museum of Indian artifacts and art, as well as a trading post featuring basketry and other Indian crafts.

FRANKLIN

Grevemberg House. Built in 1853, it hosts a large collection of paintings, artifacts, and antiques, including antique children's toys.

Main Street. Row after row of nineteenth-century restored homes, most private, can be seen during a drive-by tour.

Frances Plantation. Built in 1820, the lower portion was made of handmade brick, the upper portion of Louisiana red cypress. It is furnished with antiques, many of which are for sale.

GOLDEN MEADOW

Petit Caporal. A 130-year-old shrimp boat is on display, named for Napoleon (the "Little Corporal") and used at one time to shrimp out of Bayou Lafourche.

Wisner Wildlife Management Area. Accessible by boat launch, the 26,300-acre area has rabbit, duck, and rail hunting, shrimp and crabbing, as well as fishing. Connected by bayous, ditches, and lagoons.

GRAND CHENIER

Rockefeller Wildlife Refuge and Game Preserve. Contains 84,000 acres of ducks, geese, coots, nutria, raccoons, muskrat, otters, and alligators. Fishing and crabbing are permitted in season. A good Cajun guide is recommended, but not offered by the refuge.

El Neuvo Constante. The first shipwreck discovered off the Louisiana coast contained artifacts, including gold, silver, copper, pottery, and armaments.

HOUMA

Annie Miller Boat Tours. Cruise through the Bayou and marshlands, seeing wildfowl and alligators.

Southdown Plantation and Terrebonne Museum. Built in 1859 with an addition completed in 1893, the plantation has 21 rooms with two massive turrets that give it the appearance of a castle.

Shrimp-Drying Platforms. Shrimp are dried on platforms and preserved by a 100-year-old method.

Laurel Valley Plantation. The largest surviving sugar plantation complex in the United States, with 76 rooms and a museum.

JEANERETTE

Albania Mansion. Built in 1837, the house features one of Louisiana's largest antique collections, with rare dolls and a three-story unsupported stairway. Lodging is in a renovated slave cabin.

Charenton Indian Reservation. A museum and crafts store features work of the Chitimacha Indians, who were the finest basket weavers of their time.

LAFAYETTE AREA

Acadian Village and Gardens. Five restored nineteenth-century Acadian homes, as well as replicas of an Acadian chapel and store, represent an early Cajun settlement, surrounded by 10 acres of gardens and wildlife.

University Art Museum. Built in the colonial Louisiana plantation style, the art center for the University of Southwestern Louisiana exhibits a permanent collection of paintings by regional Cajun artists.

Jim Bowie Museum. A nineteenth-century Acadian house filled with memorabilia from the Alamo hero, who grew up in the Cajun city of Opelousas. Also holds other relics and artifacts from early settling of St. Landry parish.

La Poussière. In Breaux Bridge, here is a place to enjoy good Cajun music and dancing in a friendly atmosphere. Open weekends and evenings.

Acadiana Park and Nature Trail. The 120-acre park is built on the site of a prehistoric Indian settlement, with a path through undisturbed bottomland forest and streams.

Lafayette Museum. Built around 1880, and once the home of Alexandre Mouton (first elected Democratic governor of Louisiana), the museum hosts an array of Mardi Gras costumes, antiques, newspapers, and historical documents. Colonial gardens are on the grounds.

LAKE ARTHUR

Locassine National Wildlife Refuge. A 31,000-acre habitat for hundreds of thousands of geese, ducks, and other waterfowl. Hunting and fishing are permitted in season.

LAKE CHARLES

Imperial Calcasieu Museum. Displays original Audubon bird and animal prints, a seventeenth-century tapestry, and historical items.

Sallier Oak. One of the oldest in the United States—over 300 years old.

Louisiana Peace Memorial. A structure 120 feet high with 46 bird-houses, built to honor Louisiana residents who served in Vietnam.

Calcasieu River Tours. Canoe tours are available to paddle deep into the Bayou and see wild animals and waterfowl in their natural habitat. Guide strongly recommended.

Sam Houston Jones State Park. 1068 acres of lagoons, nature trails, and dense woods. Cabins and boats can be rented.

MAMOU

Fred Tate's Lounge. Every Saturday morning Revon Reed hosts a radio broadcast of live Cajun music over KEUN. The entire program is in Cajun-French.

MARKSVILLE

Marksville Indian Mounds and Museum. A series of Indian mounds along picnic grounds, with a natural history museum. The mounds hold buried evidence of a culture that flourished some 2000 years ago.

MORGAN CITY

Swamp Gardens. Guided tours through a living museum, complete with alligators, moss-covered cypress trees, and a cypress houseboat from the early 1900s.

NEW IBERIA

Justine Plantation and Bottle Museum. Built in 1822, the house has Victorian antiques and antebellum memorabilia. Next to it is an old country store built in the 1890s, with an extensive collection of antique bottles.

Shadows on the Teche. One of the state's most authentically restored and furnished homes, restored during the 1920s, it has entertained such celebrities as Mae West, W. C. Fields, H. L. Mencken, and Henry Miller.

Armand Broussard House & Mintmere Plantation. Authentic early Acadian home built in 1790 of mud and moss; has original doors, mantels, and handmade wrought iron, as well as Civil War memorabilia. Overnight accommodations on the plantation are available.

Gilbert Oak. Tree planted in 1831, one of the oldest of its kind in America, fills an entire lawn. It is covered with fern and Spanish moss.

Konriko Company Store & Rice Mill. Replica of old-time store featuring Cajun crafts, food, and other Cajun items. The rice mill began operating in 1912, and is said to be the oldest still in operation in America.

OPELOUSAS

Jim Bowie Museum. Museum hosts memorabilia of the Alamo hero who was born in the Acadian city. Also contains Acadian folklore, old manuscripts, pictures, guns, and tools.

PLAQUEMINE

E. B. Schwing Memorial Library and Carriage House Museum. Library houses a Louisiana collection. Museum is a completely furnished antebellum law office and courtroom.

Chapel of the Madonna. Said to be the smallest church in the world, only 8 feet square and accommodating only three people. The original chapel was destroyed in a hurricane. The present chapel is kept locked, but a key is left outside the door.

RAYNE

Petitjean Crawfish Farm. By appointment only, but visitors can see how Cajuns catch, peel, and cook the feisty mudpuppies.

Chretien Point Plantation. Built in 1831, the mansion is considered one of the finest older homes in the United States. Its stairway was the model for Tara's in *Gone with the Wind* and was once a meeting place for pirate Jean Lafitte.

SABINE

Sabine National Wildlife Refuge. Nearly 143,000 acres, the refuge is one of the primary waterways for wildlife in the Mississippi Flyway.

Largely marshland, ridges, and wooded islands with more than 300 varieties of birds.

ST. MARTINVILLE

St. John Plantation. Built in 1828 and still a working plantation, visitors can see it from Highway 347.

Longfellow Evangeline State Commemorative Area. This 157-acre park on the banks of Bayou Teche features an eighteenth-century Acadian home and "Evangeline Oak," made famous in Longfellow's poem. The home is filled with antiques and is restored to its original condition.

St. Martin de Tours Catholic Church. Along with stained-glass windows from 1765, the old church contains relics and antiques. The grave and a statue of "Evangeline" (Emmeline Labiche) are in the church graveyard. The nearby Petit Paris Museum houses old bottles, dolls, Mardi Gras costumes, and artifacts of the region.

SIMMESPORT

Yellow Bayou Historical Civil War Memorial Park. The last official battle of the Civil War was fought here. Some original battle fortifications remain, and battlefields are being fully restored.

Spring Bayou Wildlife Management Area. Wildlife in its natural habitat lives on 11,600 acres, with 40 percent underwater and 70 percent submerged during high-water periods. The only entrance to the interior of the bayou is by boat.

THIBODAUX

Lafourche Parish Courthouse. Built in 1856, the courthouse features massive fluted columns and Italianate windows. The roof is made of copper domes.

Acadia Plantation. Three cottages built on the site by Jim Bowie in the 1820s were joined with a Victorian-style facade in the 1890s.

VACHERIE

Plantations. The town is filled with old, restored, pre–Civil War plantations, most privately owned, but all visible on a drive-by tour through the town.

VILLE PLATTE

Miller's Lake. Boats can be rented for some of the finest bass fishing in the area.

Louisiana State Arboretum. This 300-acre park located within Chicot State Park contains 100 specimens of native plant life along nature trails.

WASHINGTON

House of History. An 1835 building, believed to be haunted.

Thistlewhaite Wildlife Management Area. 11,000 acres of bottomland forest and wildlife, with hiking trails.

Festivals

CAJUNS HOLD FESTIVALS for practically everything they do, have been through, or like to eat—rice festivals, oil festivals, crawfish festivals, freedom festivals. In all, there are 91 different fairs and festivals in Acadiana. (It's hard to keep an accurate count because every year, it seems, Cajuns find something they forgot about and hold a festival for it!) Every town in southern and southwestern Louisiana has its own fair or festival. The smaller towns put just as much work into their festivals as the bigger towns. Almost every town spends the entire year planning for the event, and just about everyone in the town contributes something.

Signs and decorations usually begin going up about a month or so before the festival, with the town really gearing up during the week preceding the big event. The roads slowly come to life as trucks haul in gallons of fresh oysters and what seems like tons of shrimp, crab, and crawfish. The main roads slowly fill with makeshift booths and tables, restaurants move tables outdoors, women make crafts to sell, and the town prepares for a wave of visitors.

People come from all over the world to some of the festivals. The Breaux Bridge Crawfish Festival is so popular that more than 100,000 visitors attend and has gotten so big that it is now held only every other year, in even-numbered years. Outsiders are never considered

166

"tourists" by the Cajuns. They're called visitors, and they're always treated as such.

Days before the festival, Cajuns begin taking bets on who will enter, who should enter, and who will win the contests—eating contests, drinking contests, tests of strength, costumes, dances. You name it, Cajuns will hold a contest for it, enter it, and bet on it. Once the Cajuns decide who will enter each contest, they get into serious training. Contestants practice peeling and eating crawfish, shucking oysters, picking cotton. Each festival is considered a sort of mini-Olympics when it comes to training and winning. For the Cajuns, there's dignity in chowing down several hundred shrimp or crawfish in record time. They also elect kings and queens of their festivals, and the title is considered an honor. Almost any Cajun will be able to tell you who was crowned Crawfish, Frog, or Cotton king or queen in any given year. And they'll be able to tell you who lost how much money by betting on the loser.

The most famous of all Louisiana festivals is the New Orleans Mardi Gras, held each year before Lent. The celebration in New Orleans is the most popular of any annual festival in America, and attracts visitors from all parts of the world. It's also the most outrageous, with a glut of tourists decked out in grotesque costumes, shoving and pushing their way to grab necklaces, coins, and flowers thrown from the floats. The streets are jammed with people going out of control. A sea of empty and confused faces trapped in a madhouse of fun.

Cajuns do participate in the New Orleans Mardi Gras, but it is not really considered part of the Cajun festivals. Acadiana is more south and west of New Orleans, and relatively few Cajuns live in the city. The New Orleans Mardi Gras is far too elaborate, superficial, and chaotic for most Cajuns, who like things just a little simpler and more natural.

Cajuns do celebrate Mardi Gras throughout Acadiana. Almost every town holds some sort of event to mark the days before Lent. Cajuns are religious, and Easter is a special, holy season for them. Mardi Gras (Fat Tuesday) is considered the last celebration before a solemn month of preparation before Easter. Each town celebrates in its own way, with parades, dances, contests, and parties. The local Mardi Gras celebrations are the only ones held in unison throughout the Bayou, but they are not a contest of "one-upmanship" among the Cajuns. Most of the participants are local, because visitors usually spend their time at the big festival in New Orleans.

During Mardi Gras, local dance halls are decorated for extra fun at the fais-dodo. The owners go all out—the Mardi Gras dances may be the last dances until Easter. Cajuns whoop it up, drinking, laughing, and dancing until all hours of the night. They set out to jam a month's worth of fun into an evening's worth of dancing. And they succeed.

Festivals are held throughout the year, with each town's major festival geared around the town's leading crop or symbol or favorite food. Cajun towns usually respect one another's choices for festivals, and will not also adopt the same symbol for their festival. Therefore, just about everything is honored in some sort of festival.

Here is a list of the more popular Cajun festivals, and the time of year they're usually held.

JANUARY

Cameron   Louisiana Fur and Wildlife Festival—Usually held in the second weekend in January.

FEBRUARY/MARCH

Acadiana   Mardi Gras—Held throughout most of the Bayou and in New Orleans right before Lent and the Easter season.

APRIL

Napoleonville   Madewood Arts Festival—Usually held in the beginning of April or the very end of March.

Welsh   Cajun Food and Fun Festival—Held toward the middle or end of the month.

Thibodaux   Thibodaux Fireman's Fair—Usually held at the end of April.

Lake Charles   Contraband Days—Held the last week of April.

Breaux Bridge   Breaux Bridge Crawfish Festival—Held only during even-numbered years, usually late in April.

MAY

Opelousas Family Spring Day—Held the last week in May.

JUNE

Gonzales Jambalaya Festival—Held the second week in June.

Galliano South Lafourche Cajun Festival—Usually held the second or third week in June.

JULY

Elton Louisiana Freedom Festival—Always held during Fourth of July weekend.

Morgan City Morgan City Fourth of July Celebration—Held during Fourth of July weekend.

Des Allemands Catfish Festival—Usually held the second week in July.

Kaplan Bastille Day Celebration—Held the fourteenth of July.

Galliano Louisiana Oyster Festival—Held in mid-July.

Norco/Destrehan St. Charles Parish Festival—Usually held late in July or early August.

AUGUST

Delcambre Delcambre Shrimp Festival—Usually held the second or third week in August.

SEPTEMBER

Morgan City Louisiana Shrimp and Petroleum Festival—Held the first week in September.

Gueydan   Gueydan Duck Festival—Held in mid-September, during hunting season.

Lafayette   Festivals Acadiens—Five festivals held at one time, usually in mid-September.

Rayne   Rayne Frog Festival—Held the third week in September, at the end of frog season.

New Iberia   Louisiana Sugarcane Festival and Fair—Usually held in late September.

Lake Charles   Southwest Louisiana Fair and Expo—Held the last week in September or early October.

OCTOBER

Raceland   Raceland Sauce Piquante Festival—Held the first week in October.

Sulphur   Calcasieu-Cameron Bi-Parish Free Fair—Held the first or second week in October as a two-parish effort.

Ville Platte   Louisiana Cotton Festival—Usually held early in October.

Abbeville   Louisiana Cattle Festival and Fair—Held early in October.

Chauvin   Lagniappe on the Bayou Festival—Held early in October.

Port Allen   West Baton Rouge Parish Fair—Held the second week of October.

Lafayette   Louisiana Oil Festival—Usually held in the middle of October.

Crowley   International Rice Festival—Usually held in the second or third week of October.

Franklin   International Alligator Festival—Usually held in the middle of October.

Mathews   La Vie Lafourchaise Festival—Held in mid-October.

Jennings   Jefferson Davis Parish Fair—Usually held in the middle of October.

New Roads Pointe Coupee Fair and Festival—Held the third or
fourth week in October.

Opelousas Louisiana "Yam"-Bilee—Usually held the last week in
October.

LaPlace LaPlace Andouille Festival—Usually held the last week in
October or first week in November.

NOVEMBER

Basile Louisiana Swine Festival—Held the first or second week in
November.

Grand Coteau Festivals de Grand Coteau—Usually held the first
weekend in November.

DECEMBER

Acadian Village (Lafayette) Christmas Comes Alive!—Held early in
December, continuing through the Christmas season.

Cajun Pronunciation Guide

IT'S A HOT SUMMER DAY. You're driving through the Bayou, looking at the water chickens and alligators, eyeing the cypress trees and the long-hanging moss. You see the sun happily bouncing off the waves of the gentle, meandering streams and swamps. You'd like nothing better than to stop and have a real Cajun meal of some hot boudin and cold coush-coush with a few crawfish at Breaux Bridge. You look at your map and find you're completely lost. There's only one thing to do: pull off the road at that little local bar to ask directions.

You turn onto a pebbly open driveway that leads to the small wooden building with the broken neon sign: Doc Thibodaux Cajun Bar and Grill. You get out of the car and notice that those pebbles on the driveway are really crushed and broken oyster shells. Inside, you see 10 Cajun men sitting at the bar, drinking beer, laughing, and talking loudly as a football game blares on the television. The men are shouting and cheering for the University of Southwestern Louisiana Ragin' Cajuns. You feel out of place, take a deep breath, and ask your question in the best way you know how: "Say, can you tell me where is Brew-ox Bridge? I'd like to get some of that bow-din and crayfish and

172

try a bit of that cow-ish-cow-ish stuff. Maybe Mister Thib-a-dukes can help. Is he here?"

You get 10 blank stares from 20 confused eyes. The men turn and look at one another, then back at you. They begin to laugh. One of the men steps forward, walks toward you, and invites you over to the bar. He sits down and you follow. The bartender slides a beer toward you. You sheepishly smile and nod, gulping your beer. Then the man leans toward you and speaks: "Mah fran. Ah tell you lookin' fer Bro Breeje. Go bag dere on de peeved rude. Leaf leff and head sowt. Go hafan owr. Den leff at de sign fer Bro Breeje. De pleet launch of craw-fish and boodahn is flin at Mulette's. Eff yer tursty, ax fer a kang of Jax, see? Pass a good time, cher."

What was that? Pass what? Go where? You finish your beer, smile, nod, and back out of the door completely confused and even more lost than when you first walked into the bar. Did you somehow cross the border? You don't remember leaving the country. Unless you've got plenty of gas, or happen to find someone in one of the larger cities who speaks more standard American English, you're lost for a long time.

When in Rome, do as the Romans do. When in Acadia, do as the Cajuns do. The first step is being able to speak the language. And the first step to speaking the language is being able to pronounce some of the more common places, names, and words.

Cajun is, of course, a derivation of French, so most of the pronunciations are French-oriented. Some letters are not pronounced at all, some are slurred together, and others have letters pronounced that are not even written. (For example, *lieux* is pronounced "loo," *choud* is pronounced "chard," and *milion* is pronounced "meeon.") The emphasis is usually put on the last syllable, but even that's not a firm rule. The best rule with Cajun is that there are no set rules. The language has been influenced by so many different cultures—French, Spanish, and English—that it's not a pure language at all.

Here are some of the more common names, places, and things in and around southern and southwestern Louisiana, along with a guide to pronunciation.

NAME	PRONUNCIATION
Alciatore	*al see uh tohr*
Amite	*ay meet*

Arceneaux	*ar sin owe*
Ardoin	*ar dwan*
Arnaud	*ar noh*
Atchafalaya	*uh chaff uh lie uh*
Aucoin	*oh kwan*
Avoyelles	*uh voils*
Basile	*bazz eel*
Beillée	*bay yayh*
Bergeron	*bair zher on*
Berthelot	*burth uh lot*
Bienville	*bee en vill*
Biloxi	*bill uck see*
Bonnet Carre	*baw nay kah ray*
Bon temps	*bonn taum*
Boudin	*boo dahn*
Bourree	*boo ray*
Breaux Bridge	*bro breeje*
Caillouet	*ky wet*
Calcasieu	*kal kuh shoo*
Carondelet	*kuh ron duh let*
Chartres	*shar tray* or *shar ters*
Chataignier	*shat taw near*
Chauvin	*shaw van*
Chenier	*shaw near*
Chicot	*shik co*
Coush-coush	*koosh koosh*
Creole	*kree ol*
Crowley	*krow kee*
Deblieux	*deb bel you*
Dejean	*duh zjawn*

Delacroix	*del uh kroy*
Delahoussaye	*del uh hoo see*
Delcambre	*del calm*
Des Allemands	*dawz all uh mawn*
Domingue	*dough mang*
Duplantier	*doo plan sheer*
Etouffee	*ay too fay*
Euchre	*you ker*
Eunice	*you niss*
Fais-dodo	*fay doo doo*
Feliciana	*full ee she ann uh*
Fontainebleau	*fon tain bloh*
Fontenot	*font in oh*
Fortier	*fohr shay*
Gaudet	*go day*
Gauthier	*go chay*
Godchaux	*god shaw* or *god show*
Goudeau	*go dough*
Gremilion	*grem e on*
Gris-gris	*gree gree*
Gueydan	*gay dahn*
Guidry	*gid ree*
Herbert	*ay bare*
Houma	*home uh*
Iberia	*eye beer ee uh*
Iberville	*eye buhr vill*
Istrouma	*iss true muh*
Jambalaya	*jam buh lie uh*
Jeanerette	*zjawn uh ret*

Labiche	*lah bish*
Lacour	*luh coor*
Lafayette	*lah fay ett*
Lafitte	*lah feet*
Lafourche	*lah foosh*
Laplace	*lah plahk*
Leblanc	*leh blahn*
Leboeuf	*leh buff*
Legendre	*leh zhawnd*
Loup-garou	*loo guh roo*
Loreauville	*loo ruh vull*
Mamou	*mah moo*
Maringouin	*mare in dwin*
Marrero	*mare row*
Maurepas	*maw ree paw*
Melancon	*mel awn sawn*
Melpomene	*mel poe mean*
Meraux	*mah row*
Metairie	*med uh ree*
Michel	*mee shell*
Michoud	*mee shoo*
Moisant	*moy sant*
Montegut	*mont eh gue*
Moreauville	*more uh vull*
Natchitoches	*nack it tush*
New Orleans	*naw luhns* or *new or lee uhns*
Opelousas	*oh puh loo sus*
Ouachita	*waw she taw*
Ourso	*oor sow*

Paincourtville	*pan kuhr vull*
Paradis	*pair uh dee*
Pedro	*pee droh*
Perez	*pair ez*
Piquante	*pick ahn tea*
Pirogue	*pie rowg*
Pitre	*pee tree*
Plaquemine	*plack uh min*
Plauche	*ploh shay*
Pointe a la Hache	*point ah la hash*
Pointe Coupee	*point kee pee*
Ponchatoula	*pon chew too lah*
Pontchartrain	*pon cha train*
Port Barre	*port barry*
Poussiere	*poo see air*
Prejean	*pray zhawn*
Presque Island	*praysk eel*
Rabalais	*rab ah lay*
Rapides	*rap peeds*
Rappelet	*rap ah lay*
Rayne	*rain*
Remoulade	*row moo lahd*
Richoud	*ree shard*
Rigolets	*rig uh leez*
Rouler	*roo lay*
Rousseau	*roo sew*
Sabine	*sab bean*
Saint Amant	*saint ah mawn*
Simmesport	*simms port*
Tangipahoa	*tan ji puh hoe ah*

Techefuncta	*chuh funk tuh*
Tchoupitoulas	*chop pee too luss*
Teche	*tesh*
Tensas	*ten saw*
Terrebonne	*tear uh bawn*
Theriot	*tare ee oh*
Thibodaux	*tib ee doh*
Traiteur	*tray tour*
Triche	*trish*
Vacherie	*vash uh ree*
Ventress	*ven tray*
Vermilion	*ver mee on*
Vidrine	*vy dreen*
Vieux Carre	*view kah ray*
Ville Platte	*vill plat*
Westwego	*west wegg oh*
Zachary	*zak kuh ray*
Zwolle	*swah lee*

It takes a while, but once you get a feel for the correct pronunciation of the Cajun names and words, you'll be able to get most pronunciations right—or reasonably close.

So when you're lost in the Bayou and need directions, check the pronunciation guide before you ask. That should get you started in at least asking the right questions. As far as understanding the right answer . . . that will take time. Cajuns have their own language and their own words for just about everything. For that, you'll need one more thing: the Cajun dictionary.

Cajun Dictionary

CAJUNS HAVE THEIR OWN WORDS for just about everything. Some are French, some English, some spoken with a Southern drawl, and some simply mispronounced slang expressions. When you hear Cajun spoken, you hear a mixture of Southern English, old-world French, and French street slang, all put together without a set of rules or any pattern.

Cajun is a language that's probably best summed up as the language of whoever is speaking it. If you lined 10 Cajuns side by side, you'd get 10 different dialects or accents, and each would probably have different words for the same things. Each would be correct, and each would be considered Cajun. Because of its vast differences and free-flowing lack of grammatical rules, the language has been impossible to standardize and write down.

Cajun cannot actually be taught. Like Cajun music, it has always been passed through each generation, on the knee of the grandparent to the grandchild. For the last two generations, the Cajun language has all but died as Cajuns felt pressure to join mainstream America. Cajuns felt that their language and various dialects stigmatized them; they wanted something better for their children. The Cajun language was outlawed and only spoken privately, dividing the language even further into subgroups and regional differences.

There are three main dialects of Cajun French: "le français de meche," called Marsh French and generally heard in the southern Bayou areas of Lafourche-Terrebonne Bayouland; "le français de grand bois," known as Big Woods French and spoken in Courtableau Country and the more wooded areas; and "le français de prairie," or Prairie French, spoken in Imperial-Calcasieu Territory. The differences are subtle, but there.

One Cajun story points out how these different dialects could result in an embarrassing situation if you're not careful. A priest from one Bayou parish visited another parish and guested on a radio talk show. He told how his parish raises money through bake sales, where the women of the parish get together every Sunday and sell their cookies on tables in front of the church. The story was harmless enough, except that "selling their cookies" in this parish didn't quite mean the same thing as in the priest's parish. Radio listeners translated the Cajun priest's story to mean something closer to prostitution! The phones rang off the hook.

Fortunately, Cajun is once again being heard throughout the Bayou and even into Texas and other parts of the South. The Cajun people are making a major effort to keep their heritage alive, although because of the ban on Cajun for so many years, damage has been done. A lot of the old Cajun has been lost, and only a minority of older Cajuns speak real Cajun-French well enough to pass it along. Most of what is now heard in the Bayou is Cajun-American, or American English spoken with a Cajun dialect and drawl.

When you've spent a little time in the region, you'll be able to pick up certain sounds and patterns in Cajun-English. Cajuns with heavy Cajun-American accents often drop the *a* on words beginning with that letter. They pronounce *th* as *d* and sometimes convolute the letters in a word or phrase. Once you've heard it for a while, it becomes clear and fun to listen to.

The following is a short guide to Cajun-English, giving some of the more common English words and one of the ways Cajuns might pronounce them. Each area has its own dialect, so there is no cut-and-dried pronunciation for most of the words. And the dictionary is all in fun. It's not meant to be a serious dictionary, but is a way to help outsiders get a sample of the flavor of the region through the spoken word. Its purpose is only to entertain.

Here are some of the more common words and phrases you'll hear in the Bayou, in conventional English and in the Cajunized pronunciation or the Cajun equivalent word.

ENGLISH	CAJUN
abdomen	admen
able-bodied	abody
about	but
absent	apsin
Acadian	cajun, coon ass
accent	axun
accident	axdunt
accordion	squeeze-box
ache	a (such as in heada, backa, toota)
act	ak
address	number or numbers
admit	mit
afraid	fray
agree	gree
alligator	gator
anatomy	antme
ankle	enkle
appear	peer
ask	ax
average	ayverge
back	bag (directional)
bait	bet
bank	bang (as in swamp)
bask	bax
bath	bat
bed	bade
belly	bailey
boil	boll
bone	boon
braid	brad

broom	brum
bury	booree
call	reach
can	cane, kang
candle	cannel
captured	cattured
carrot	keert
cast	cass
catch	kitch
chocolate	jake-a-lit
confederate	kinfedderd
conjure	conjoe
cost	coss
cypress	cypurse
dead	dayed
dependable	penbull
dialect	dyelick
dog	dowg
double	dubba
drawbridge	drawberge
dumb	thick
each	itch
earn	earin
earth	ert
egg	ayg
either	edder
entertainer	ennertanner
exercise	exsize
eye	ah
factory	fackree
family	people
fast	fass

father	fodder
feather	fayder
festival	bal
field	petch (land)
filling	flin
footrest	fooress
friend	fran
gate	get
general	genreal
get	git
granddaughter	granoughta
grandfather	granfodder
grandmother	granmudder
grandson	grans'n
greedy	kletchy
gulf	guff
hair	harrs
head	hayed
hell	hail
help	hep (hepped)
here	cher, cheer
horse	hoss
hot pepper	hop-epper
hungry	honegree
I	Ah
ideal	ahdull
ill	eeall
incantation	gris-gris
indigestion	injettin
interest	innerst
introduce	make a meet
iron	ion, arn
jar	jaw
July	Julee

junior	junya
juvenile	juvnull
kept	keeped
kitchen	ketchun
land	place (property)
large	big big
leap	lep
leave	leaf
left	leff
leg	lag
lift	liff
like	lak
locust	lacuss
lost	loss
Louisiana	Loozeeann
lunch	launch
magazine	magzin
merchant	murshawn
mind	myn
murky	thick
my	mah
nail	nall
naked	neck't
nasty	bad way
native	nave
nest	ness
north	nort
number	numah
nutria	nutra, neutral
obligation	oblayshun
occult	conjoe
oil	all

old	o'
osmosis	ozmose
overrun	runover
oyster	oysuh
oyster cracker	oysuh crackah
pack	peck
paper	pepper
party	bal
past	pass
pasture	pasteer
pave	peeve
personal	parsunel
phone	harn, squawk box
pig	peeg
plate	pleet
plenty	plenny
plump	thick
pole	poll
popular	poplah
post	poss
predict	purdik
punch	pawnch
question	keshtin
quilt	kilt
rabbit	raybid
raccoon	coon
radio	rayjo
record	raycurd
red	rad
regular	reglure
right	rat
road	rude
root beer	roobur

run	ruin
salt shaker	saljar, salbox
same	sem
sauce	salz
school	skull
scratched	kretched
second	sekun
self	seff
senator	sent'r
shrimp	shrimps (always pl.)
soft	soff
south	sowt
spoil	spull
stretch	stritch (measure)
surveyor	server
swat	swat (*a* as in *cat*)
talking	tak-tak
teacher	titchur
teaspoon	tesspin
the	de, da
theirs	deres
then	den
there	dere
this	dis
tolerance	tolernce
touch	tetch
trouble	terbble
turkey	turnkey
unanimous	unimous
unbroken	unbroke
under	unner
vacuum	vack'em
vegetable	vegable

very	varry
violent	violet
voyage	vodge
wait	wade
wander	wanner
weather	wedder
wicked	wicker
winter	winner
witch	wish
with	wid
wolf	woof
X-ray	eggs-ree
year	yur
yellow	yalla
yesterday	yestiddy
zero	zurrow

PHRASES

back here	bag dere
call me	reach me
carport	car porch
cotton field	cotton patch
exit left	leaf leff
from here	from dese parts
have fun, dear	pass a good time, cher
oil field	all patch
over there	or dere
remove	take bag
swamp bank	swam bang
today	now-a-days

turn around   come 'round
unite   tie loose
wait here   wa cheer
who's that   who da
your family   you people

Talking Cajun

Now THAT YOU KNOW A FEW CAJUN WORDS and how some of the names and towns are pronounced, you're one step closer to deciphering some of these strange and wonderful-sounding sentences and sayings you're bound to hear on your travels through the Bayou.

Here are some Cajun sentences, written in dialect as they'd probably sound deep in the Bayou, along with the "American" translation. (Most French or Cajun-French has been left out because of its complexity.)

Cajun
"Ah et too menny mudpuppies, and now mah bailey's sore."

Translation
"I ate too many crawfish, and now I have a stomachache."

Cajun
"A new all petch peered in da swam bang, or dere cross de guff."

Translation
"There's a new oil field in the swamp, over there across the gulf."

189

Cajun

"Ah need sum abody coon ass to hep catture de neutral who runover de pasteer."

Translation

"I need an able-bodied Cajun to help me capture the nutria that have overrun the pasture."

Cajun

"Mah hoss break his leff enkle boon and now he's dayed. Ah booreed him bag dere a stritch affer de skull."

Translation

"My horse broke his left leg, and now he's dead. I buried him behind the school."

Cajun

"De gators is hidin unner de cypurse. Ah tell dem to git, but ah think dere's gonna be terbble, so Ah ax mah people to come round from dere."

Translation

"The alligators are hiding under the cypress trees. I tried to get rid of them, but I think there's going to be trouble. I told my family to stay away from there."

Cajun

"Yestiddy Ah saw de wish in de swam. Ah was honegree, so she conjoed some vegable salz in her ion pot. Ah keeped a jaw of de conjoe in my ketchun. Et was good."

Translation

"Yesterday I visited the witch in the swamp. I was hungry, so she mixed some vegetable sauce in her iron pot. I now keep a jar of the mixture in my kitchen. It was good."

Cajun

"Let me make a meet wid de sent'r, sos Ah can ax him when de server's gonna look over dis here fackree. Ah don myn watin, but it's puttin me in a bad way."

Translation

"Let me introduce myself to the senator, so I can ask him when the surveyor will take a look at the factory. I don't mind waiting, but it's putting me in a nasty mood."

Cajun

"De Loozeeann dyelick is hard to learn, but you kin git it ventully lak ozmose if you try."

Translation

"The Louisiana dialect is hard to learn, but you can pick it up eventually, almost through osmosis, if you try."

Cajun

"You have no oblayshun to eat oysuh crackah wid de shrimps. But you gonna like de boll keert and jake-a-lit milk. If you et too much, you git injettin, so don git kletchy."

Translation

"You have no obligation to eat the oyster crackers with the shrimp. But you are going to like the boiled carrots and chocolate milk. If you eat too much, you'll get indigestion, so don't get greedy."

Cajun

"De squeeze-box player is absin. Ahm fray he kitched a hayed cold and is feelin eeall."

Translation

"The accordion player is absent. I'm afraid he caught a head cold and is feeling ill."

Cajun

"Junya has a innerst in big big cotton petch bag dere. So Ah gotta titch 'em to be a reglure Loozeeann farmer."

Translation

"Junior has an interest in a large cotton field back there. So I have to teach him to be a good Louisiana farmer."

Cajun

"De storm is thick and dark lak lacuss peerin on mah place. Ah knew Ah edder get hep or loss mah pasteer."

Translation

"The storm was black and dark as if locusts had appeared on my farm. I knew I either had to get help or lose my pasture."

Cajun

"Reach me at da murshawn. Ah git mah harrs cut after dinner."

Translation

"Call me at the general store. I'm getting a haircut after lunch."

Cajun

"It was an ahdull gris-gris dat was put on de o' woof. He ain't been bag in a yur."

Translation

"It was an ideal spell that was put on the old wolf. He hasn't been back in a year."

Cajun

"Leaf leff, unner de peeve drawberge. Don go fass or de pleece will ketch ya."

Translation

"Exit to the left, then go underneath the paved drawbridge. But don't go too fast, or the police will catch you."

Cajun

"Mah granoughta ak fray of da loup-garou. So she hid unner de bade till de wicker conjoe leaf cher."

Translation

"My granddaughter was acting afraid of the werewolf. So she hid under the bed until the wicked incantation left here."

Cajun

"De Kinfedderd army wind de war. Dey gonna catture de Nort again. Ahm gonna git mah people fighting. Mah granfodder was a genreal."

Translation

"The Confederate army will win the war. They're going to capture the North again. I'm going to get my family to fight. My grandfather was a general."

Cajun

"Ah have haff a myn to write de magzin and newspepper. Dey purdik de new raycurd gonna be poplah rat cher, when de singer ain't a reglure Cajun."

Translation

"I have half a mind to write the magazine and newspaper. They are predicting that the new record will be popular right here, when the singer isn't even a regular Cajun."

Cajun

"Jo-Jo Thibodaux's goin to git the numbers on Tchoupitoulas, and buy some dubba hop-eppers and pawnch for de fais-dodo."

Translation

"Jo-Jo Thibodaux is going to get the address on Tchoupitoulas, and buy some double hot peppers and punch for the Saturday night dance."

Cajun

"Ah gree. Mah fran made a reglure peeg outta hisself wid dat roobur and boll ayg dinner. It's gonna spull his supper!"

Translation

"I agree. My friend made a regular pig of himself with that root beer and boiled egg lunch. It's going to spoil his supper!"

Cajun

"Take a tesspin of medicine to take bag a cold. Git in bade till your heada goes."

Translation

"Take a teaspoon of medicine to get rid of a cold. Get in bed and stay there until your headache goes away."

Cajun

"You can pass a good time wid a kang of Jax and a pleet of mudbugs, jus sos you don shuck dem hayeds till deys bolled."

Translation

"You can have a good time with a can of Jax (beer) and a plate of crawfish. But be sure not to suck the (crawfish) heads until they are boiled."

Cajun

"Mah fodder works at da fackree in de day, and he's an ennertanner at de bal at night."

Translation

"My father works at the factory during the day, and he's an entertainer at the festival during the night."

Cajun

"Ah keeped the juvnull outta mah ketchun because Ah was jawin some gator salz."

Translation

"I kept the juvenile out of my kitchen because I was putting up some alligator sauce in jars."

Cajun Names

ACCORDING TO AN OLD CAJUN LEGEND, a person can become a Cajun in only three ways—by birth, by the ring (marriage), or through the back door. The back door is simply moving to the southern or southwestern Bayou areas, accepting the Cajun lifestyle, and living with the Cajuns. Many outsiders, or visitors, are considered full-fledged Cajuns after living in the Bayou only a few years.

One thing that sets Cajuns apart from the rest of the people in the area is their heritage, most obviously seen in their French (or Spanish) last names. (Many Spanish names came from the early days when Louisiana was settled and ruled by Spain. Although these people are not actually Cajun by birth—they are not full-blooded Acadian—they are considered Cajun either because of the intermixing of the Spanish and the French, or because they've lived in the Bayou for many years.)

About 5000 Acadians originally settled in Louisiana, the majority from the same families. Those first families established the region, settled it, turned it into a prosperous area, and multiplied. New Acadians flocked to the land, adding new families to the roster. Families intermixed and grew. Today there are hundreds of Cajun (and almost Cajun) names scattered throughout the Bayou. But the names of the original families that settled the area and started towns in the region are still the most common names in southern and southwestern Louisiana.

Here are some of the more common names you'll find in the Bayou. Once you become familiar with the list, you'll be able to recognize a Cajun and get a sense of how the first families have grown and spread throughout the region.

Alexander	Comeaux	Jennings
Allain	Cormier	Juneau
Alleman	Courville	Labbe
Ancelet	Credeur	Lacombe
Ancoine	Daigle	Lafleur
Arceneaux	DeBlanc	Lagneaux
Ardoin	Delacroix	Lambert
Arnaud	Delahoussaye	Landry
Aucoin	Delcambre	Langlinais
Babin	Delhomme	Lantier
Babineaux	Desormeaux	Latiolais
Badeaux	Doucet	Lavergne
Barrilleaux	Dugas	LeBlanc
Baudoin	Duhon	Lormand
Beaullieu	Duplechin	Louviere
Begnaud	Dupre	Malveaux
Benoit	Dupuis	Marceaux
Bergeron	Etienne	Mathews
Bernard	Fontenot	Matthews
Bertrand	Fournet	Mayeaux
Billeaud	Fruge	Meaux
Blanchard	Fuselier	Meche
Bordelon	Gaspard	Melancon
Boudreaux	Gauthier	Mouton
Boudro	Gautreaux	Narcisse
Bourgeois	Girouard	Olivier
Bourque	Glaude	Patin
Breaux	Goudeau	Pellerin
Broussard	Guidry	Perrodin
Carreire	Guilbeau	Picard
Chaisson	Guillory	Pierre
Champagne	Herbert	Pitre
Chauvin	Henry	Plaisance
Chiasson	Jagneaux	Plouet

Prejean
Primeaux
Prudhomme
Quebodeaux
Rabalais
Rabeaux
Reaux
Richard

Robicheaux
Rousseau
Savoy
Senegal
Sonnier
Stutes
Theriot
Thibeaux

Thibodeaux
Touchet
Trahan
Vallier
Veillon
Vermilion
Vidrine
Vincent

CONCLUSION

Bayou Changes

THE BAYOU—THE LAND AND ITS PEOPLE—is continually undergoing change. Only the future will know if the changes are for the better, but even in an area where the pace slows down and time gently walks instead of runs, change is inevitable.

The Bayou area was once wilderness, overrun with wild plant life; all kinds of wild animals roamed through the Bayou; the waters were filled with different types of fish and shellfish, spilling over the banks. Cypress once blanketed the entire Louisiana forest region, crowded together with oak, pine, and gum trees. Homesteaders who came to the Bayou ran small farms and raised large families. The soil was rich; corn, rice, potatoes, pecans, sugarcane, and indigo grew in abundance. Cattle roamed freely. Then the Bayou began to change.

Lumber companies swarmed to the area, ripping up trees, chopping down timber, leaving many once-full areas barren and dead. Oil companies moved in, digging up fertile land for speculation and drilling. Factories sprang up; the once-peaceful and calm Bayou became riddled with people scrambling to find their place. The area seemed to begin to fall out of balance. People were exposed to the outside world during World War II, especially Cajun men who were shipped around the country and the world to fight. When they returned home, they felt out of place; the Bayou suddenly seemed backward and ignorant. Cajuns started rejecting their background and French heritage, forbidding French to be spoken. They felt like outsiders, and were looked on as "poor white trash" because of their rural life-style and broken English. They wanted to fit in with the rest of the country, and not stand out as backward.

The land was in danger of being ravaged; the people were in danger of losing themselves and fading into oblivion. Something had to be done, but it took two generations before a move was made to stop the exodus. Cajuns began working with the companies that infiltrated their land and helped the companies prosper; the area turned into one of the most productive and lucrative in the South. They worked *with* nature, replacing trees, fishing and hunting in selected seasons, drilling and pumping in certain areas. The damage to the land has been repaired. Unfortunately, that isn't the story with the Cajuns themselves.

Cajun-French has never really been written down, and it was never taught in the schools. It was a dialect that was learned in the home, and learned only by being exposed to it. That home exposure was cut off for two generations, and Cajun was not spoken except by a handful of Cajuns who refused to knuckle under to pressure to change. CODOFIL instigated a program teaching French in the schools, but the French is textbook French, not Cajun, and most Cajuns believe the step is nothing more than a nice gesture that is too little too late. Most Cajuns say the language is as good as dead. As it dies, so dies a major part of the Cajun culture. A culture that is unique in America— part of our country and our history—should be looked on as significant, but the important effort to save it doesn't seem to be there outside of the Bayou. The fight to revive the Cajun culture is neither greatly funded nor promoted outside of southern and southwestern Louisiana, and the push from within is led by only a handful of Cajuns.

Today, Cajun music and Cajun cooking are the two key elements that are keeping the Cajun culture afloat. As the music spreads throughout the country and embraces a larger and larger audience, mainstream America will begin to learn about the Cajun people and their background. The wonderful Cajun food will spark an interest in Acadiana and the Bayou. Once outsiders find out about that special group of people living in a magical, wonderful place, they'll discover the Cajun's secret to happiness. Balance and harmony, living with nature, and letting the good times roll.

Laissez les Bons Temps Rouler!

BIBLIOGRAPHY

BOOKS

Broven, John, *South to Louisiana, the Music of the Cajun Bayous*, Pelican Publishing Company, 1983.

LeBlanc, Dudley J., *The True Story of the Acadians*, Dudley LeBlanc, 1932.

Rushton, William Faulkner, *The Cajuns, from Acadia to Louisiana*, Farrar, Straus & Giroux, 1979.

Hunter, Theresa M., *The Saga of Jean Lafitte*, The Naylor Company, 1940.

Tisch, Joseph LeSage, *French in Louisiana*, A. F. Laborde and Sons, 1959.

PAMPHLETS

"Acadian Profile," Cajun Country Tour Guide and Louisiana's French Heritage, Box 52247, Lafayette, LA 70505.

"Evangeline," Evangeline Advertising & Printing, Simmesport, LA 71369.

"River Trails, Bayous and Back Roads," Louisiana Office of Tourism, P.O. Box 44291, Baton Rouge, LA 70804.

"Conversational Cajun French 1," Pelican Publishing Company, Gretna, LA 70053.

Miscellaneous handouts, one-page articles, and flyers from the Louisiana Office of Tourism and the Lafayette Chamber of Commerce, Lafayette, LA 70503.